estherpress

Books for Courageous Women

ESTHER PRESS VISION

*Publishing diverse voices that encourage and equip women to walk
courageously in the light of God's truth for such a time as this.*

BIBLICAL STATEMENT OF PURPOSE

*"For if you keep silent at this time, relief and deliverance will rise for the Jews from
another place, but you and your father's house will perish. And who knows whether
you have not come to the kingdom for such a time as this?"*

Esther 4:14 (ESV)

What people are saying about ...

Each One Reach One

"Whether on a platform before thousands or over a cup of coffee with only one, Babbie Mason lets her heart for the Lord shine through. For more than three decades, my life has been personally impacted by the intentional way this woman has chosen to reflect the light and love of Christ through the words she says, the attitude she exudes, and the character she demonstrates. I'm so glad she has penned her thoughts and insights on how we can do the same."

Priscilla Shirer, Bible teacher and author

"Jesus said that believers are the light of the world. So, just how do we shine His light to others so He gets all the glory? Babbie Mason knows how. *Each One Reach One* is a biblical resource packed with encouragement and ideas for loving others well and reaching the world for Jesus. If you long to make a difference doing kingdom work with kindness, this is the book for you!"

Karen Ehman, *New York Times*–bestselling author, international speaker, and Bible teacher in the First 5 app

"There are people who craft and perform songs that move you. There are speakers who bring truth to life in ways that cause you to lean in. There are authors who put pen to page to tell their stories in ways that pull you out of complacency and call you higher. There are believers who walk the talk day in and day out. And then there's Babbie Mason, who does *all* that with the ease of your best friend over coffee. I've loved her for many years and am the recipient of her warmth and wisdom. This book is about sharing your faith in an 'everyday' way. You will find yourself stirred, strengthened, and grateful on every page."

Anita Renfroe, comedian, author

"*Genuine, gentle,* and *inspiring* are all words that speak to me of Babbie Mason and her heart for the Lord. Her latest, very practical study of Matthew 5:16 will take you on a journey she has walked herself as she has learned to bring light to dark places and offer hope to those who are barely hanging on. Once you experience God's Word through Babbie's eyes, you will find a renewed enthusiasm to share with your world that God is faithful and, in Christ, everything is going to be alright."

Jan Silvious, speaker, author of *Courage for the Unknown Season*

"Join Babbie Mason as she teaches you how to lead a life that makes a difference. Read amazing stories of random encounters that turned into astounding miracles, along with how you can walk in this same power of God's love. *Each One Reach One* is a must-read for anyone who wants their light to shine the hope of Jesus Christ into the lives of others."

Linda Evans Shepherd, bestselling author of 38 books including *Praying through Hard Times* and host of the *Prayer Investigator* podcast

"If you sense your light has dimmed or could shine a little brighter, this book is for you! I deeply admire Babbie Mason's passion for Jesus and the many ways she uses her gifts for His glory. Whether singing, speaking, writing, or hosting TV and radio shows, she humbly ushers a bit of heaven down here to earth. Babbie is truly a beautiful, bright light. In this very relatable book, she offers practical ways for each of us to "turn up the voltage" in our everyday living. Plug into *Each One Reach One* so that you, too, can be part of God's chain of events—a powerful chain that can never be broken."

Ellie Lofaro, author, Bible teacher, international speaker, founder of Heart Mind & Soul Ministries

"I met Babbie Mason nearly forty years ago at a Christian songwriters' conference. Since then she has been a dear friend, a songwriting mentor, a spiritual support, and an amazing role model. I have long called Babbie a master storyteller, a claim she lives up to exceptionally well in this book titled after her iconic song "Each One Reach One." With rich scriptural references and practical exercises, *Each One Reach One* is both an enduring and endearing guide for living. Babbie urges us to trust God in all things and to always pray for and share Christ with others. Her insightful revelations will surely have a lasting impact on the heart and life of every reader and encourage each one to reach one!"

Carol Ross-Burnett, EdD, distinguished toastmaster (Toastmasters International), singer-songwriter, author, speaker, and founder of the Platform Workshop for Christian Artists

"Brace yourself for impact! *Each One Reach One* is a book God will use to speak to us all. From presidents to prisoners and all the way to the checkout line at the Piggly Wiggly grocery store, life is about serving people for the Lord. I laughed. I cried. I gave God the glory. Each chapter is challenging and chock-full of wisdom and faith. I found myself inhaling the words and exhaling the praise!"

Tammy Whitehurst, speaker, writer, and Jesus follower

"I am excited about Babbie Mason's book *Each One Reach One*. Babbie shares the love of God in such a warm and loving manner that people are drawn to her and their hearts are open to hear her testimonies of faith. I believe this book will encourage people to share God's love with those they meet in their day-to-day lives, whether inside the grocery store or outside in the parking lot. Babbie Mason is more than an award-winning singer and songwriter; she is a woman of God and a friend to all who are blessed to know her."

Cydney Wayne Davis, singer, songwriter, vocal coach, and producer

"*Each One Reach One* is a beacon of inspiration for Christians seeking to fulfill the call of Matthew 5:16. With practical wisdom and heartfelt encouragement, this book empowers readers to illuminate their circle of influence with the radiant light of Christ. A must-read for anyone eager to make a meaningful impact in their daily life by spreading God's love and truth with grace and authenticity."

Angela Alexander, inspirational speaker
and author of *Miracles in Action*

"If you've ever struggled with how to share your faith in Christ, then Babbie Mason will inspire you with a can-do attitude. After reading Babbie's book *Each One Reach One*, I'm more motivated than ever!"

Wanda Obermeier, award-winning
author of *Mama Bird Papa Bird*

"In this timely book, Babbie Mason presents practical ways to share our faith without the dread or anxiety that can often accompany our efforts to do so. This is a must-read and a must-do that motivates us to joyfully fulfill the Great Commission through our everyday encounters and interactions."

Deborah Smith Pegues, bestselling author
of *30 Days to Taming Your Tongue*

"Babbie Mason's beautiful book *Each One Reach One* is packed with encouragement and backed with truths from God's Word. Her many stories resonated with me, and I found myself both laughing and teary-eyed as I read them. This excellent, thought-provoking guide shows us how to shine for Jesus and glorify His name. It's easy to understand and provides strong 'doables' for growing our faith and reaching others for Christ. Babbie's love for each reader is evident, and her heartfelt remembrances are a testament to God's faithfulness—proof that we too can each reach one."

Carole Brewer, author, singer-songwriter, and podcast host

Each One Reach One

Babbie Mason

Each One Reach One

Everyday Ways You Can Shine God's Light

Reflecting Matthew 5:16

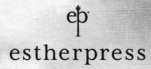

esant herpress

Books for Courageous Women
from David C Cook

EACH ONE REACH ONE
Published by Esther Press,
an imprint of David C Cook
4050 Lee Vance Drive
Colorado Springs, CO 80918 U.S.A.

Integrity Music Limited, a Division of David C Cook
Brighton, East Sussex BN1 2RE, England

Library of Congress Control Number 2024931077
ISBN 978-0-8307-8566-7
eISBN 978-0-8307-8572-8

The Team: Susan McPherson, Marianne Hering, Judy Gillispie,
Kristen Defevers, James Hershberger, Susan Murdock
Cover Design: James Hershberger

Printed in the United States of America
First Edition 2024

1 2 3 4 5 6 7 8 9 10

050624

Meet the Author

The name Babbie Mason is synonymous with creative excellence. A two-time Dove Award winner, Babbie has written songs that have been published in more than twenty-five languages and are featured among the great hymn writers and their timeless compositions. Many of her musical works are considered modern-day church classics.

Babbie's music is a mainstay on radio, television, the internet, and the silver screen, including Denzel Washington's blockbuster film *Déjà Vu*.

She is also a speaker and the television talk-show host of *Babbie's House*. As an author, Babbie writes Bible studies to challenge others to develop an intimate relationship with Jesus Christ. A dedicated teacher and women's conference speaker, Babbie encourages women to find identity through the love of Christ.

Babbie Mason is a cheerleader for up-and-coming creatives, mainly music artists, songwriters, and self-published authors. Babbie shares her global platform (BabbieMasonRadio.com) with independent singers, songwriters, and authors who wish to communicate their music, books, and God-stories with the world. She also teaches students in the college classroom, serving as artist-in-residence and adjunct professor of songwriting at institutions such as Lee University in Cleveland, Tennessee, and her alma mater, Spring Arbor University in Spring Arbor, Michigan.

Babbie is recognized in the Christian community for her encouraging lyrics and resplendent music, yet she remains approachable, and she humbly acknowledges her blessings come from God.

She and her husband, Charles, are the parents of two adult sons. They live on a farm in Georgia where they enjoy family, fishing, eating fresh from the garden, stargazing, and sunsets. Learn more about Babbie at www.babbie.com.

To my sons, Jerry and Chaz,
whose laughter will always
be music to my ears.

Contents

Foreword

We have all met someone whose light was so obvious that we prayed they would always be in our life. That's how I felt when I heard and met the brilliant Babbie Mason at a women's retreat. I was the speaker, and she was contributing the music as well as being the one who drew the audience into the warmth of her melodic heart. Babbie's gift of kindness shines through every note she sings, every spoken word she shares, and every noun she writes, her favorite noun being *Jesus*.

Years have gone by and, praise God, Babbie has remained in my life for over three decades at this writing. During that time I have had the good fortune to watch her faithfully walk in the light of Christ's love toward countless attendees. And I've had the joy of seeing how she heaps admiration and encouragement on her family and somehow still has an abundance for her friends.

In this world of troubles, to find a circle where you feel seen and safe is rare. Babbie offers that. She draws her circle with room for the bruised, the broken, and the maligned. In all the years I've known her, I cannot remember a time when I heard her speak ill of anyone. Really. Now that's admirable. Nor have I ever heard her complain about exhausting travel schedules or ministry demands. Now, c'mon, that's not just rare—it's miraculous.

The high quality of how Babbie conducts herself makes it worth it for us to studiously examine her written and spoken offerings; it's an investment in our own growth. She knows what she speaks of when she says "Each one reach one," because Babbie's been doing exactly that most of her life. She knows that the more we step outside the claustrophobic circle of ourselves to include and care about others in ways that matter, the wider our hearts will become and the brighter our lives shine.

Bring a sharp pencil when you read, watch, and listen to Babbie, because it's been my experience you'll want to take notes. There are also soul-searching questions throughout the book that are definitely worth our writing time. She offers these to help us process truth in our inward parts and not just let them skid through the freeway of our busy brains.

Along with all Babbie's other gifts, she has the gift of grocery shopping. That is a gift, isn't it? Trust me, it *is* when you shop with Babbie! Ask the customers, the checkout clerks, and the stock people where she shops—they know. Read on; you'll see. Babbie has never met a stranger.

Babbie knows how to care for our weary hearts with her life-enriching music and her passion for the light in God's Word. She's a woman of prayer and praise who is continually on the lookout for God's kind hand, strong voice, and loving heart.

So here's my suggestion: Pull on your friendliest jammies (mine have polka dots), pour a cup of tea (herbal for me), fluff your pillows (I use three), lean back, and prepare to be blessed, gently instructed, and deeply comforted.

Patsy Clairmont
Conference speaker and award-winning
author of *God Uses Cracked Pots*

Introduction

W hile writing this book, I crossed a major threshold in my life. Sixty years ago, I accepted Jesus Christ as my Savior. Growing up in a Christian home, I never thought of myself as anything but a Christian. As a child I made a public profession of my faith in Christ. I was only eight, but I was old enough to understand the importance of my decision.

Ten years ago, I reached what I call my Year of Jubilee—the fiftieth anniversary of giving my life to Christ. I was speeding headlong toward my sixties and approaching thirty years in ministry. For almost four decades, I had worked hard to achieve career milestones. I'd written chart-topping songs and recorded several music projects. I'd won music industry awards and performed before millions of people through concerts, radio, television, and audio-video content posted on the internet. But concerning my personal walk of faith, there was still something missing.

During that season of reflection, I had an epiphany: the years behind me were more than the years in front of me. I wanted my life, my faith, and the rest of my years to really count. As a follower of Christ, I wanted to live my faith out loud, with more boldness, more purpose, and more intention.

So I prayed this simple prayer:

Lord, will You give me more opportunities to share my faith with others, even when I'm not onstage? Everywhere I go—to the post office or the grocery store, to the doctor's office or the airport—help me share the love I have for You with a contagious joy and a confident faith. If You open a door, I'll shine my light, share my faith, and walk through it. Amen.

In my heart, I believe God was waiting for me to pray that prayer! And He took me up on it. Almost immediately, He began to place me in situations where I could tell others about the love of Christ. Countless opportunities arose where I could be a witness for Him. As a result, God began to show up and show out in incredible ways as He placed me in the path of people who needed a light to shine on their hopeless circumstances.

It was clear. God wanted me to shine my light with more passion and purpose. God desires to use you in the same way. That's why I wrote this book. If you are a believer in Christ Jesus, I'm inviting you to join me in lifting the light of the gospel higher than we have before. It is a privilege to lead you through an inspiring adventure, where together we will discover the call, the responsibility, and the joy of reaching our family, our friends, and even strangers with the gospel message. At the outset of this adventure, I hope you will be motivated to pray a simple prayer of your own. Ask God to give you opportunities where you can shine your light for Christ and change your world one encounter at a time.

You may choose to use this book, *Each One Reach One*, as a personal evangelism tool. As you read, be open to personal challenges and introspection, and pay special attention to areas in your life where you can grow and advance in sharing your faith. Or you may choose to invite a small group of friends to journey with you. Then you can share your experiences together. Either way, as you read, write, pray, and imagine, I am trusting God to speak to your heart. I will be praying that you will allow God to increase your passion to shine your light and reach out to others with the gospel in ways you never thought possible.

My Story

As a pastor's kid, I saw my parents' faith in God demonstrated through their many years of dedicated service. If someone in our church or community was not walking with the Lord, my parents knew how to lead that person to Jesus. If a church family member was sick or hungry, or needed employment, counseling, or help of any kind, my parents were there to tirelessly meet or advocate for those needs. In other words, my parents were all things to all people that they might win some (see 1 Cor. 9:22). The spirit of faith and optimism was always present in our home. That hopeful spirit deeply impacted and shaped my four siblings and me. Many of the life lessons I learned from my parents were taught, but most of them were caught. I knew God was real and that integrating faith and service could change hearts and lives. I saw my parents share their faith in tangible ways right before my eyes on a daily basis. As a young believer, I wanted my parents to be proud of my Christian service, but I was also beginning to realize that my service to God was a way I could give Him glory with my life.

Serving God has been a way of life for me since my conversion. Sharing my gifts and talents wherever I can brings me incredible joy. In church or school, in business or pleasure, if I can be a blessing to someone with a word or a song, then give me the stage. Blessing people through words and music is something I believe I was born to do. Throughout my life and ministry, I've spent countless hours onstage performing for people. After my appearances, people often tell me how much they enjoy what I do.

Having spent years and years hearing comments and compliments, you might think it all goes straight to my head. But the opposite is true. The words go straight to my heart. They speak life to me and help to establish my destiny. I taught middle-high school music and English for years. But my husband, Charles, reminds me often that I didn't quit teaching school; my classroom just got bigger. I can't imagine doing anything other than encouraging people.

Author, pastor, mentor, and my good friend Jason Perry says in his book *A Word to the Wise*: "Bloom where you are planted. Instead of lamenting about where you are not, decide to use the time and resources available to you where you are to help you become who God created you to be."[1]

Anyone who is associated with a Black inner-city church knows that blooming where you are planted is considered an art form. The Black church has always been the perfect environment to develop creative resources. Besides my father, there were no full-time paid staff members in our thriving neighborhood church. My father's salary was meager compared to the financial packages many pastors receive today. We weren't rich by any means, and we certainly didn't live an extravagant lifestyle. But the Lord supplied what we needed. My mom and dad were serial entrepreneurs. My three brothers, my sister, and I seemed to catch that spirit. Even as kids, we all had part-time jobs. There was always this underlying attitude in our family that you must work hard and "give it all you've got." That work ethic has shaped me to this day.

Everyone in our family was encouraged to contribute their gifts to the church and the community in some way. When my parents discovered I could play a few chords by ear on the piano, I was hired to fulfill all the duties as the church pianist at age nine. (Yes, I said *nine*!) The day I accepted that enormous responsibility, I felt as if God had thrown me into the deep end of the pool without a life preserver. Even then, I understood the critical need for a church musician. Because our church congregation and choir members didn't read music, I sometimes fumbled at my attempts to play all the songs by ear. I didn't have much experience, but I didn't see anyone else stepping up to assume the role, so I jumped in wholeheartedly.

With the Lord's help, years of piano and voice lessons, and an abundance of encouragement from church and family members, I grew in my musicianship. I became proficient in singing, playing the piano, rehearsing, and directing all the choirs that sang throughout the month in our Sunday morning worship services. I served in my father's church for nearly twenty years. The foundation of the ministry I am enjoying today was established in that life-giving community.

The gift of music God gave me flowed naturally and blended with the duties that were placed upon me at the church. I sat perched on the bench behind a huge upright piano, which gave me the best seat in the house. It was undeniable. From that vantage point, I saw the love of Jesus revolutionize the lives of everyday people who sat in those church pews. As a result of my father's sound gospel preaching, I could see the evidence of God's power in transformed lives. One of the greatest ways to lead others to Christ is to live a godly life before them. It was easy to follow Christ because I watched my parents talk the talk and walk the walk.

> **Like adding kerosene to a blazing fire, God was increasing my passion to reach others for Christ.**

The Mississippi delta has produced some amazing people: blues legend B. B. King, legendary opera singer Leontyne Price, and media mogul Oprah Winfrey. My paternal grandfather, Pastor John Wade, also hailed from the Magnolia State. The son of a preacher and the grandson of slaves, he led four congregations in the Mississippi delta, visiting each congregation one Sunday a month until he went home to be with the Lord at age eighty-four. And my parents, Willie and Georgie Wade, left Mississippi during the Great Migration in the mid-1940s to settle in southern Michigan. Shortly after their arrival, my father founded the Lily Missionary Baptist Church in Jackson, Michigan. My parents led the church for nearly forty years until my dad went home to be with the Lord. My relatives may have considered themselves ordinary, but to me they are giants in the Hall of Faith. Certainly, I have big shoes to fill and a great heritage of faith to live up to.

My relatives were a great example for me as I endeavored to define my faith. They faced tremendous adversity, maneuvering racism, economic challenges, threats to religious freedom, and raising a family during the turbulent sixties and seventies. They were overcomers in every sense of the word.

Growing up in a generation influenced by "drugs, sex, and rock 'n' roll," I found my own life being shaped by cultural and political pressures. When I became a young adult in the seventies, it wasn't as easy to stand up for Jesus outside the walls of my father's church. Even though I was a preacher's kid and a young Christ follower, I often found it difficult to be a good witness for Christ. I felt ill equipped to merge my faith and my culture as I tried to navigate the Black power movement, the women's liberation movement, the peace movement, and even the Jesus movement. Later on, ministry as a Christian singer and songwriter gave me the platform to share my life stories from the stage. I have always been comfortable onstage. I had difficulty, however, finding the right words or recalling the right "formula" when it came to witnessing with people one on one.

Quite often while participating in church services or reading inspirational books and magazines, I'd learn how others witnessed for Christ and led their peers or family members to the Lord. I was jealous of their zeal and of how effortless sharing the gospel seemed for them. I desired that kind of passion. Even then, I realized that God, in His faithfulness, had been shaping my life's story. More and more I heard people share how my music, books, and spoken messages had brought them to faith in Christ and helped them to mature in their faith. Like adding kerosene to a blazing fire, God was increasing my passion to reach others for Christ.

Shine for Him

By the time I reached my fiftieth year of walking with Jesus, I was ready to face that moment of crisis. I called out to the Lord with my heartfelt prayer. Here's how that prayer became a reality in my life: First, I realized my prayer was actually a prayer of surrender. I chose to submit my life totally to Christ. I traded my desires for His. Gradually, He began to teach me how to love Him more deeply.

Second, as a result of rededicating my life to Jesus, an interesting phenomenon began to take place. It became easier to love other people too. I became more keenly aware that God's presence was living in me through the Holy Spirit. His light began to shine with more intensity in my life. His power was giving me more boldness. His words became a part of my conversations. His love was changing me, and I wanted to impact my world more than ever—onstage or one person at a time.

Third, I realized the choice was mine. I could be satisfied with my life and say, "I'm happy with the way things are. Evangelism is not my job. Besides, sharing the gospel is awkward. Leave that to pastors, Bible study teachers, and other ministry professionals.... Me? I can never seem to find the right words. Let someone else do it." I did not want that to be my story, and I did not want that omission on my spiritual record.

Reaching this conclusion drove me to action. I chose to recognize the biblical reality that people the Lord allowed me to influence could actually have their names written in the Book of Life if I told them about Jesus. I concluded that though I don't have all the answers and I'm not a theologian, I wouldn't let that stop me from sharing what I already know to be true right now. A particular evangelism formula might escape my memory, but I can easily tell others how Jesus changed my life. I may not be a persuasive apologist, but I can love others to Jesus with a heart of kindness, care, and compassion. First Peter 3:15 became my heart's desire: "Instead, you must worship Christ as Lord of your life. And if someone asks about your hope as a believer, always be ready to explain it" (NLT).

With that inspired mindset, it didn't take me long to discover that when people are desperate, they will reach out for something or someone to hold on to. There have been countless times when I have asked a stranger how they were doing, and they opened up to tell me their problems. I didn't dismiss them; I leaned in and listened.

When that happens, I encourage people and follow the Holy Spirit's direction as I bring Jesus into the conversation. With the Holy Spirit's guidance and the love of Jesus, I just take a little time to care. I can easily love people and be a lifeline for those in need of hope. The old adage is true: people don't care how much you know until they know how much you care.

Maybe you are facing a critical place in your journey where you feel compelled to be more intentional concerning your faith. Do you want to be more vocal in telling others about Jesus? Is it your desire to be more involved in leading others to faith in Christ? Or maybe you have had opportunities to share your faith but fear won out and you chose to say nothing. It could be that you are sharing the gospel with others but you're not seeing the results you hoped to see. If you want to shine your light a little brighter and share your faith with more passion, this book will serve as a guide to help you become more sensitive, more compassionate, more confident, and more purposeful in being a witness for Jesus.

Shining your light doesn't mean you'll step up on a soapbox, grab a megaphone, and preach a sermon, although God calls some to do that. But it does mean you will probably go out of your way more often to be a blessing to strangers. You will become more intentional about sharing the gospel with your neighbors. It also means you will take the liberty to tell someone about the Lord while standing in line at the pharmacy or the grocery store checkout lane. Instead of being abrupt, irritated, or curt, you may find the opportunity to be a little more thoughtful to the customer service agent after you've waited on the phone for too long, listening to that annoying hold music.

It means you will make it a practice to speak to people, look them in the eye, and ask how they are doing. And when they share a slice of their life, you'll take a moment to listen and show them you care. You may even be called upon to step out of your comfort zone and pray for someone in the doctor's office waiting room, airport gate area, or city bus. Some may see these moments as interruptions or inconveniences. But I've found that every unexpected opportunity and every people encounter is a divine setup, presenting us with the opportunity to share the love of Christ with someone who is lost, hurting, or discouraged.

In these pages, we'll look at Matthew 5:14–16. I call this passage the Great Mandate because it's an official command from Jesus to shine our lights before others—*on* purpose, *with* a purpose, and *for* a purpose—all for the glory of God. We'll examine the entire passage. Then, in phrase-by-phrase fashion, we'll focus on verse 16, to apply the principles of this key verse to our own lives. We'll look at each word to determine how we can fulfill that mandate.

Jesus spoke the words from Matthew 5 around two thousand years ago. Each word is still timeless and timely. I am one whose life has been turned around by the message of the Great Mandate. As God speaks to you, I believe there is no way your life can remain unchanged. You will hear some of my own incredible God-stories that are sure to encourage you. Each encounter contains a valuable lesson that motivated me to give my light away. I hope they inspire you too.

Let me suggest that you keep a record of your own God-stories. Write them down in detail. Then review them from time to time to encourage yourself in the Lord. Share your testimonies with friends, on social media, in your email, on your blog or podcast. Just get the word out that Jesus is the light of the world. With all my heart, I believe your own God encounters are on their way!

Right now, read the words of Jesus from Matthew 5:14–16:

> You are the light of the world. A city that is set on a hill cannot be hidden. Nor do they light a lamp and put it under a basket, but on a lampstand, and it gives light to all who are in the house. *Let*

your light so shine before men, that they may see your good works and glorify your Father in heaven.

We'll look at each phrase of the Great Mandate with the goal of applying each phrase personally and purposefully. Here's the ground we'll cover during our *Each One Reach One* encounter:

1. Jesus is the light of the world.
2. Humans are innately sinful. We live in and love darkness.
3. When we come to Christ, our lives are transformed and filled with the light of Jesus.
4. We are the reflection of Jesus. We are to shine with intensity before others and be intentional about it.
5. Our good works allow people to see that living for Jesus is the only way to enjoy life to the fullest.
6. God chose you for a work that will require use of your heart, your head, and your hands. You can use all your gifts and talents to lead others to Christ.
7. Everything you do for Christ matters. The light you shine has a never-ending impact. A life of obedience to Christ matters because shining your light has eternal implications—for you and for everyone you encounter.
8. When we shine our lights, we make God look good.

On the Journey Together

To say I'm excited about this message is an understatement. I am overjoyed to share with you how God placed me in the path of people who needed a light to shine on their dark existence. But most of all, I consider it a privilege to lead you through a deeper understanding of God's Word, where together, we will discover the wonderful privilege of reaching others with the gospel of Jesus. I hope you will be motivated to pray a simple prayer of your own. As you do, ask God to give you opportunities to shine your light and change your world one encounter at a time.

Are you ready for an adventure of a lifetime? Not just a faith adventure for a few weeks, but a life-changing commitment of shining your light? According to Matthew 5:14–16, your life and your light are intertwined. They are inseparable. John 1:4 says, "In Him was life, and the life was the light of men." *Light* in this respect doesn't mean photons emitted by the sun or the glowing filament of an incandescent lamp. The light of Christ is alive and personal. His light shines through your life. Our relationship with Jesus changes everything. The truth of God's Word opens our eyes. When we accept Jesus as Savior, we see and comprehend His truth for the first time. In the light of Jesus, we breathe in new life. And that new life influences everything we do. Every kind word shines a light. Every good deed shows the way. Every person you meet will say there's something different and attractive about you. Get ready to place your light high on a lampstand and shine for the ones you'll meet along the way!

To close this introduction, I would like to share one of the first amazing encounters I experienced after praying and asking God to help me shine my light.

One evening on the way to a celebration for a friend, I stopped at a Sam's Club to pick up a bouquet of flowers and a greeting card to give her as a gift. I'd never shopped there before, but I reasoned that the store carried what I needed. Once inside, I flagged down a clerk who took me to the flower department, and I chose a beautiful bouquet. Next, I grabbed a congratulatory greeting card, and in no time at all, I stepped into the checkout lane.

The clerk then said, "Now, you're going to need your Sam's Club membership card."

"This is my first time in the store," I replied. "I don't have a card."

"Well, you won't get the club discount. You'll just have to pay full price."

With a bit of relief in my voice, I said, "Hey, at this point, it is what it is. I'm just happy I found what I need."

That's when a nice lady stepped into the line behind me. She'd apparently overheard the conversation. She jumped in and said with a lilt in her voice, "If you'd like, you can use my card. Then you can get the discount!"

I was more than happy to accept her offer. The gentleman ahead of me had a huge cart of groceries, so I relaxed and leaned in to the conversation. "Why, thank you, my dear friend! God bless you!"

"Child, I need a blessing," she immediately responded. "My grandkids have moved in with me, and they're about to eat me out of house and home. I have a thirteen-year-old grandson, and that young man is keeping me on my knees."

In an effort to encourage her, I said, "Well, I just pray then that God will open up the windows of His heaven and shower down so many blessings upon you and your grandkids, you won't have room enough to receive them all."

That dear lady was running with that blessing before I could get out all the words. She lifted up her hands and began to praise God right there in the checkout lane. She exclaimed, "Thank You, God. I need that blessing! Thank You, Jesus! I receive that blessing!"

I jumped right in along with her. "Amen! Thank You, Lord! Thank You for blessing my friend!"

This moment was natural and spontaneous. We were just two strangers, two sisters in the Lord, enjoying God's presence in the checkout lane of Sam's Club.

I suddenly realized that a second young woman had stepped into the lane. She caught my eye, motioned to me, and said, "Excuse me, ma'am. But if you don't mind, could I speak with you for a moment?"

I was a bit surprised but not the least bit hesitant. I stepped around the first woman, who still had her hands lifted, engaged in praise, and I went to the second lady. "What can I do for you?"

She replied with great sincerity, "If you don't mind, would you bless me too?"

At that very moment, I sensed the Holy Spirit's presence. I knew down in my heart that He was orchestrating those moments.

Recalling Proverbs 3:5–6, I said, "Oh, precious one. The Lord loves you so much. He has a wonderful plan for your life. And, yes, He does want to bless you. He wants you to live for Him and trust Him with all your heart and lean not to your own understanding. But in all your ways acknowledge Him and He will direct your path. Do you believe that?"

Tears welled up in her eyes and streamed down her face. She nodded, acknowledging her belief. That young woman reached out to hug me. She clung to me like a long-lost friend. As she held on, I prayed a soft, simple prayer: "Dear Father, thank You for allowing me to meet this precious young lady. Help her to live for You with everything inside her. In her searching, thank You for being the answer to all of her questions and for supplying all her needs. In Jesus' name, amen."

We were just two strangers, two sisters in the Lord, enjoying God's presence in the checkout lane of Sam's Club.

It was then my turn to check out. So I pushed my cart forward and paid for my items. I waved goodbye to my new friends and headed toward the exit where an attendant waited. He sat on a tall wooden stool behind a narrow desk, and his job was to check my items against my receipt. After he finished his task, I turned to leave the store and was a few steps away when he stopped me. "Excuse me, ma'am," he called. "Before you go, if you don't mind, would you bless me too?"

I laughed heartily and returned to his desk. I recalled the blessing from Numbers 6:24–26 and prayed with all sincerity, "My dear brother, I pray that the Lord will bless you and keep you. May He make His face shine upon you and be gracious unto you. May He lift up His countenance upon you and give you peace. Do you receive it?"

With a hearty voice, he said, "Amen, I receive it."

I felt lighthearted and amazed by what had just happened. Yes, I needed flowers and a card. But more than that, people inside that store needed the light and the love of God to shine upon their worlds, wherever they were coming from or going to. From that moment on, I became more aware than ever that God orders our steps so we can shine His light. According to Psalm 37:23, "The LORD directs the steps of the godly. He delights in every detail of their lives" (NLT). I don't have to be concerned about who I will reach or how I will shine my light. Neither do I have to be concerned about the outcome. All of that is His doing. I left Sam's Club with a gift for my friend and a gift from God. I was determined to let go of my inhibitions and let God show the way. He knows how to guide me and the direction I should take. Life is much more exciting when I walk by faith, trusting God with every step.

As you read this book, I'll be asking you to make yourself available to God. With whatever gift you have, I fervently hope you'll allow God to use it to love others, bringing the attention and the glory to Him. I'm excited that you are reading these pages, and I'll be praying for you as you dive into the deep end of God's love for you. It's from the overflow of your love for Jesus that your light shines. Indeed, let me pray with you right now.

Dear heavenly Father, thank You for this grand opportunity to explore what it means to be a light that shines for You. Open our eyes to the possibilities and encounters that await us as we share our faith with others. I know You see and understand the heart of my dear friend who is reading this book. Help her to see with deeper insight, to comprehend with greater clarity, and to trust with firmer faith, knowing that You are with her at every intersection of her life's journey. Lord, You know this dear one by name. Thank You for her sensitive heart and her willing spirit. Alleviate her fears and replace any reservations she has about sharing her faith with a sense of anticipation along with an unction of urgency and boldness she has never realized. Please allow Your light to shine in, around, and through her so others may see Your life in hers, thereby giving You glory. Speak to her on every page. Remind her that she is deeply loved, greatly blessed, and highly favored. We're excited for the outcome! In Jesus' name, amen.

How to Use This Book

Each One Reach One is divided into eight chapters. In each chapter, we'll examine Matthew 5:14–16 to discover biblical principles to help you share your faith in Christ with passion and confidence. Whether you read a chapter a day on your own or a chapter a week with a small group, you'll find spiritual truths you can readily apply.

To begin each chapter, watch the video session. Then, once you've finished your reading, use a journal to write down answers to the questions at the end of each chapter. Also use your journal to record the names of those you want to see come to know the Lord. Create a special section for those friends and loved ones you are praying for and hope to lead to Jesus. This will also be where you can write the God-stories that are sure to take place. Review and share those God-stories from time to time to encourage yourself and others.

Access the vidoes here:

Search https://davidccook.org/access/
Use access code: EachOneReachOne
Or scan this QR code:

Chapter 1

Your Time to Shine

*You are the light of the world—like a city on a hilltop
that cannot be hidden. No one lights a lamp and then
puts it under a basket. Instead, a lamp is placed on a
stand, where it gives light to everyone in the house.*

Matthew 5:14–15 NLT

Imagine what the world was like before there was light. The earth was empty, dark, and desolate. There was no plant life, no food, and no oxygen. The sky was black, and the oceans were lifeless. There were no fish, birds, animals, or flowers. There were no people. No family. No you.

Then God said, "Let there be light." Suddenly the whole world came alive with beauty and splendor. Everything began teeming with life. Since that moment, the world has never been the same. The magnificent power and undeniable presence of light immediately burst upon creation. The Bible says the originator—the personification of light—is God Himself. God doesn't need the sun, the moon, or the stars, for they are only His instruments of light. God does not merely represent or reflect light. The Bible doesn't say that God has access to light. The Bible says that He *is* light.[1]

The light of God brought His glory and wonder into the world, illuminating His beauty and perfection to all humankind. Light reveals God's goodness and shines upon all the amazing things He has made. God holds the trademark as the sole proprietor of light and all of this wonderful creation He shines upon.

A few years ago, I heard someone quip, "There is so much darkness in the world, somebody ought to do something about it." Well, God did do something about it. He made us to be "light." We have the blessed privilege of being used by God to usher His light into the world. When we shine for Jesus, darkness doesn't stand a shadow of a chance, but it must acquiesce to light at every opportunity. Let's look at our key verses for this chapter, Matthew 5:14–15, to get a glimpse of God's plan for combatting the darkness:

> You are the light of the world. A city that is set on a hill cannot be
> hidden. Nor do they light a lamp and put it under a basket, but on a
> lampstand, and it gives light to all who are in the house.

As believers in Christ Jesus, our mission is to shine in a world where we are surrounded by spiritual darkness.

Let me tell you about a time God used me to light up a place in my community, a time when He placed me "on a lampstand."

My husband, Charles, and I were looking forward to having a few friends over to our home for dinner. As the date for the dinner party grew closer, just thinking about all the preparations overwhelmed me because I'd recently spent time on the road, appearing at concerts and speaking engagements. With limited time on my hands, I decided to solicit some help from a friend who owns a southern barbecue restaurant near our home.

A couple of days later, I dropped by the restaurant to discuss some menu options with the owner. While we were talking, a young lady who was sitting at the restaurant counter looked up and spoke to me.

"Excuse me," she said, "but are you a gospel singer? Don't you have a television talk show? I think I've seen you on TV."

I affirmed her questions, smiled, and introduced myself.

She placed her napkin beside her plate and said, "I love your music. Would you sing something for me right now?"

Her request surprised me, but it didn't catch me off guard. For me, singing a song for someone is never an inconvenience, so I complied without a hint of hesitation. I lifted my head, raised my hands, and began singing out a chorus of the popular hymn "How Great Thou Art."

While I was singing, I looked around the small dining room and noticed people looking up in response to the song. Gradually, I moved to the center of the small lobby, as if I were moving to the center of a stage. While I continued to sing, a few men removed their ball caps. Other customers laid down their forks and lifted their hands in worship as a holy hush fell across the small, quaint dining room.

With my face toward the heavens, I lifted my hands and ended on a high note. The room erupted with applause as I smiled and thanked everyone. But that's not the half of it.

Right after I wrapped up my conversation with the proprietor, hugged her neck, and turned to leave, the cook came out of the kitchen. She wiped a bead of perspiration from her brow and a trail of tears from her eyes. She stopped me before I could open the door, calling out to me, "Excuse me, Babbie. Can I speak with you for a moment?"

I stepped back and turned toward her. "What can I do for you, my friend?"

She took me by the arm and ushered me aside. Speaking softly, she said, "Thank you for singing that song. I really needed to hear that message. Some days I feel so low, I can hardly find the strength to get out of bed and feed my three kids. At night I pray, and I wonder if God can even hear me, 'cause it seems like my prayers don't even make it past the ceiling. Then you came in here and sang that song. I *know* God sent you in here just for me. I believe He wants me to know that He is hearing my prayers. Your visit lets me know God is with me and I'm not alone after all."

I wanted to melt into the floor after hearing her heart. We wiped away our tears as I reached out to embrace her. I took advantage of the moment to pray with her as I tucked a small financial token of love into the pocket of her apron. There was no doubt in my mind that God had sent me on a mission. I was full, and I hadn't even eaten a bite.

> ## When we shine for Jesus, darkness doesn't stand a shadow of a chance.

God's Love Story

People are looking for that type of hope-filled experience. The whole world is craving an encounter with God's love. He wants to use you and me as conduits so that He might overwhelm us with His love in such a way that we don't have room enough to receive it all. God has this way of multiplying our blessings above and beyond anything we could imagine. Being so full because of His blessings, we must give some of His love away. Ephesians 3:20 beautifully sums up how God chooses to use us: "Now to Him who is able to do exceedingly abundantly above all that we ask or think, according to the power that works in us."

The story of God's love is so incredible and yet so easy to understand that one Bible verse (I think of it as the Golden Text) can summarize it: "For God so loved the world that He gave His only begotten Son, that whoever believes in Him should not perish but have everlasting life" (John 3:16). This verse may seem overused. But don't allow its familiarity to deter you from understanding its critical meaning. God poured out His love to such a great degree that He gave us the very best gift He had. He gave us Jesus, His only Son. The fact that anyone can know Jesus is the best news we could ever hear. *And* the best news we could ever share.

Your testimony is your story of how God's unconditional, sacrificial love has changed your life. Your testimony is your God-story. It is not meant to be kept a secret. It's meant to be shared. In fact, God created you to introduce His light to the world. *You* are the light of the world.

The headlines in our news feeds remind us just how dark the world is becoming. There is no better moment than right now for you to shine. You are that lampstand referenced in Matthew 5:15. It's time for you to hold your light high so others can see it. Just think how God can use the power of your light to overcome darkness. Think how your light can reflect Christ so He can reveal His truth and save the lost. The presence of your light has the ability to overcome hatred, divisiveness, and confusion and bring peace into any situation.

Take the Message Everywhere You Go

Your personal God-story is a love story that is unique to you. The problems you've endured or the heartbreaks you've faced are formative, but they're not the center attraction. Your God-story is not about your problems. It's about the answers that Jesus has provided you. Always remember this: Whatever the question is, the answer is Jesus.

Telling others the Jesus-story has always been the main event. Jesus wants everyone to know that they matter to Him. No matter who you are, where you come from, or what your story may be, you are welcome in the family of God.

That message deserves to be told. And multitudes are waiting to hear it. In New Testament times, there were no cell phones or televisions. And, of course, the internet didn't exist. Back then, the best and only way to get the good news of the gospel to those who needed to hear it was by telling the story of Jesus to one person at a time. That method works just as well today as it did back then. God uses people to spread the message of His saving grace. He uses people like you and me to evangelize the whole world and spread the gospel like a wildfire. That's right. Each one can reach one!

When Jesus delivered the Sermon on the Mount, He wasn't speaking to a forum of college students seeking to earn their master's degrees in theology. When Jesus spoke His famous last words of the Great Commission, He didn't address learned global church dignitaries. Jesus invited people from all walks of life to follow Him. Once they became Christians, they were to tell others about their faith in Christ. That's how the message was spread. There wasn't a plan B. There never has been. Plan A has always been to include you in perpetuating Jesus' message.

Jesus' first disciples were ordinary men who caught smelly fish for a living. You can't get any more ordinary than that! Jesus compelled them to follow Him, saying, "Follow Me, and I will make you fishers of men" (Matt. 4:19).

I trust you are leaning in right now with your ear to God's heart. He is speaking to you as well. You may follow your favorite people on Instagram or YouTube. You may stay glued to your phone to hang on to every word your favorite cultural celebrities have to say. Allow me to encourage you to make Jesus the one you follow first and most of all. He says, "Come, follow Me, and I will make you fishers of people." Follow on, my friend. Follow on!

A Surprising Evangelist

As you let Jesus Christ lead, you are leading the way for others. You are to "do the work of an evangelist" (2 Tim. 4:5).

You may wonder if you fit the description or if you are cut out for that assignment. One of the first evangelists was not a pastor, preacher, or paid professional but a common, ordinary person of low social standing. This person was one of Jesus' most dedicated followers, having been present at many crucial points of Jesus' earthly ministry. She was a woman named Mary Magdalene. Luke 8:1–3 tells us that Jesus delivered her of seven demons, miraculously releasing her from demonic oppression and torment. This event changed her life so drastically that she became a dedicated follower of Jesus and contributed her financial resources to support His ministry.

Mary Magdalene remained faithful to Jesus even in His darkest hours. All four of the Gospels testify of her presence as she and other women with similar life stories followed Jesus everywhere. She was most likely present to witness Jesus' teachings. No doubt she witnessed Him—exhausted, bloody, and beaten—laboring to drag a heavy cross through the streets on the way to Golgotha's hill. The Bible records her presence at the crucifixion and the resurrection of Jesus. The highlight of Mary Magdalene's story takes place at the empty tomb. (No disrespect to the disciples is intended here; however, Mary Magdalene demonstrated herself faithful to Jesus while the disciples were hiding out in fear for their lives.) It was Mary Magdalene, accompanied by other women, who attended to the body of Jesus at His burial. She discovered the empty tomb that first resurrection morning. It was Mary Magdalene who led the disciples back to the empty grave. After the men had left and gone back home, Mary Magdalene had an amazing encounter at the garden tomb, as recorded in John 20:15–18 (NLT):

"Dear woman, why are you crying?" Jesus asked her. "Who are you looking for?"

She thought he was the gardener. "Sir," she said, "if you have taken him away, tell me where you have put him, and I will go and get him."

"Mary!" Jesus said.

She turned to him and cried out, "Rabboni!" (which is Hebrew for "Teacher").

"Don't cling to me," Jesus said, "for I haven't yet ascended to the Father. But go find my brothers and tell them, 'I am ascending to my Father and your Father, to my God and your God.'"

Mary Magdalene found the disciples and told them, "I have seen the Lord!" Then she gave them his message.

Running back from the grave to find the disciples, Mary was the first to proclaim the exciting words, "I have seen the Lord!" You see, the first-century explosion of the gospel was in part due to enthusiastic preaching by great teachers such as the apostle Paul. But as the message of Jesus began to be preached outside of Jerusalem in densely populated places such as Ephesus, Corinth, and Philippi, it was ordinary people who took the message and ran with it, spreading the gospel to thousands, then millions, of broken, hurting people who were perfectly positioned and ready to receive the good news. You and I are a part of that chain of events.

Our Part of the Chain

We are all called to be evangelists. Did you know that? An *evangelist* is someone who seeks to convert others to the Christian faith. The word means "one who proclaims good tidings."[2] So what can we learn from Mary Magdalene, this dedicated follower of Jesus?

We Are to Be Tenacious

First, we see that Mary Magdalene was *tenacious* in her pursuit of Christ. She was eager to learn from Jesus and determined to follow Him for the rest of her life. After all He had done for her, dedicating her life to Him was the least she could do. Mary was relentless in her pursuit to know Jesus, to love Him, and to worship Him. She knew that real worship is not just acknowledging Jesus as Savior but surrendering to Him as Lord. She followed Him everywhere and supported His ministry with the works of her hands and her financial resources. From the onset of Jesus' ministry to the bitter end, this woman was there, relentlessly pursuing her Lord and Master, Jesus the Christ.

This shows us that it takes persistence and determination to follow Jesus. It takes serious resolve and purpose to commit to being a true child of God. Christianity is not for the indecisive. We must make up our minds whose side we are on. Don't give it a second thought when it comes to leaving your old life behind to forge ahead to a new life in Christ. For sure, you will come face to face with disappointment. But when you do, don't back down. Stand strong. Then defeat, like a wounded bully, will turn and go home. First Corinthians 16:13 gives us encouragement when it says, "Be on your guard; stand firm in the faith; be courageous; be strong" (NIV).

We Are to Be Courageous

Second, Mary Magdalene was *courageous*. With fearless fortitude, she did whatever was necessary to sit at the Lord's feet, regardless of the opposition. The fear of what others might say about her did not intimidate her. The fear of men, who may have viewed her as a liability, a weakness, or an inconvenience, did not cause her to be afraid. Neither did the fear of unworthiness cause her to retreat, for she knew what her life was like before she met Jesus. To her, Jesus made all the difference. She knew the apparent risks of following Jesus, that He was a religious and political threat. But that didn't keep her from committing to Him regardless of the cost. In ancient Jewish culture, women were not often in the forefront of public life, nor were they given much status in patriarchal society. But this was not the way Jesus viewed women. He honored them and gave women a prominent place in His ministry.

Have you ever been tempted to back down from a difficult decision because of fear? Standing up for Christ may not always be easy. We can live fearlessly in a chaotic world because we know we are not alone, for God is with us. Living for Christ in the midst of a crazy world is not just a future expectation; it is a present reality. Romans 12:1–2 from *The Message* describes living for Christ in detail, so we'll end this section with the apostle Paul's advice:

> So here's what I want you to do, God helping you: Take your everyday, ordinary life—your sleeping, eating, going-to-work, and walking-around life—and place it before God as an offering. Embracing what God does for you is the best thing you can do for him. Don't become so well-adjusted to your culture that you fit into it without even thinking. Instead, fix your attention on God. You'll be changed from the inside out. Readily recognize what he wants from you, and quickly respond to it. Unlike the culture around you, always dragging you down to its level of immaturity, God brings the best out of you, develops well-formed maturity in you.

We Are to Be Expeditious

Third, but certainly not least, Mary Magdalene was *expeditious*. After the Sabbath, she wasted no time rushing to the grave of Jesus to attend to His body with spices (Mark 16:1–3). While it was still dark, Mary Magdalene made haste to visit the tomb on that Sunday morning. In John's depiction of the story, after finding the tomb empty, "she came running to Simon Peter and the other disciple, the one Jesus loved, and said, 'They have taken the Lord out of the tomb, and we don't know where they have put him!'" (20:2 NIV).

After she had seen Jesus standing outside the empty tomb, and even spoken to Him, she found the disciples at once. She was quick to tell them the good news that Jesus was no longer dead, but He had risen just as He had said.

Mary Magdalene never doubted that Jesus was who He claimed to be. The fact that she was living a life free of demonic oppression was the only proof she needed. Jesus could heal the sick and set the captives free. She knew about those miracles firsthand. She had seen them with her own eyes. She *was* a miracle story. Wherever we find her in the Scriptures, she assumes the role of a faith-filled believer in Jesus. Following Jesus had become dangerous, and many who were associated with Him quickly abandoned Him. While Judas betrayed Jesus and Peter denied Him, this woman was stalwart in her convictions. She never gave up serving Jesus. Seeing Him endure suffering certainly weighed upon her heart and caused her great distress. But she still believed Jesus was the Messiah, the Savior of the world.

> **No matter who you are, where you come from, or what your story may be, you are welcome in the family of God.**

What can we learn after surveying the life of Mary Magdalene, the faithful New Testament evangelist? Take a look around you. Think about your home life, the places where you work or volunteer, the marketplace where you spend your money, the political arena where public policies are formed in education, sports, and entertainment. Can you imagine a place in your community where your light can shine? Do you see the need for an evangelist? Don't allow that big, traditional-sounding word to intimidate you. Own it, my friend. Tag—you're it!

No doubt, you can serve as a mouthpiece and declare that Jesus is light for this troubled generation. You've got a story to tell! This is no time to delay or hesitate. Get your story together. Muster up the courage. Make up your mind. Put on your gospel running shoes and be about your Father's business. Every believing woman should be excited about promoting the gospel and telling others about Jesus.

Nervous? Afraid? Gather some strength from Mary Magdalene. Not once did she question her decision to follow Jesus. Neither did she allow the culture of that day to shape her thinking or change her mind about where she stood. She didn't think twice about what people thought of her. But she focused on her mission—telling people about the resurrection of Jesus Christ.

You Are the Light of the World

Telling people about Jesus has been my mission and my vocation for four decades. As a Christian singer, songwriter, author, and speaker, I travel quite a bit. It's quite common for me to pack my bags and head to the airport to catch a flight to sing or speak at a church or conference in various parts of the world. When I travel by airplane, I book a window seat whenever possible. That way I can gaze at the world below. The mountains, oceans, cities, and farmlands all look remarkably different from the air. The view appears distinctively beautiful at night. I can easily see the glow of streetlights, park lights, traffic lights, automobile lights, and billboard lights as they illuminate the landscape below, making details all stand out against the darkness. I can tell whether we are flying over a densely populated metropolis or a small farm community. From the air, it's easy to determine whether the thoroughfares on the ground are expressways, city streets, or winding country roads. At night, I can easily locate the Statue of Liberty in the New York Harbor. Atlanta's city skyline, with its tall skyscrapers, is stunning against the night sky. The Ambassador Bridge to Canada is a beautiful reminder that I'm just minutes away from seeing my family in Detroit. When lights shine against the night, everything is clearly defined.

How is this possible? It's possible because the old saying is true: "The darker the night, the brighter the light." That is exactly what happens when you demonstrate the light of Christ. Like a neon sign, the transformative power of the Holy Spirit enables you to stand out, dispelling the darkness around you. This power is not given so you can make a name for yourself. God allows you to stand out so you can attract others to the love of Christ, showing them the way to Jesus.

You see, the Holy Spirit empowers you as a witness. He will give you words to speak at just the precise moment. He will lead others to you who need to know Him. The Holy Spirit will also give you boldness to tell others about Jesus. God works the same way today as He did in the first century.

A small light can illuminate a dark room. It's not about the grandeur of your light but rather the sincerity of your faith and how you live it out in your daily life. Your light can, and no doubt will, inspire and influence those around you. It can even motivate a ripple effect, reaching lives in ways you may not even know.

In Luke 8 we find that Jesus' followers were both men and women. Verses 2–3 specifically mention some followers by name. There were many other followers who remain nameless. But they are still important to the mission and the message of Christ. Everyone plays an important role. If you feel your light is small or insignificant, remember that every tenacious act of love, every courageous gesture of kindness, and every expeditious act of faith matters. Embrace each opportunity to do your part in reaching the world where you live, no matter how small the action or gesture may seem to you. Be faithful to do what God has called you to do. This is where your faith comes into play as you trust God to do what only He can do. You are making a difference.

This Little Light of Mine

Those who follow Jesus, like Mary Magdalene, are always ready to speak a word for Christ. Little did I know an unexpected opportunity to share the love of Christ was waiting for me just a few minutes from home. One day I decided to make a spontaneous visit to a local department store. Once I was inside, I grabbed my cart, intending to make a quick dash down my favorite aisles. Just then an older lady, probably in her midseventies, came through the door. I couldn't help but notice her. This spry senior citizen was styling and profiling from head to toe. She wore a plaid wool skirt and matching jacket in autumn colors with a coordinating blouse. Her outfit was perfectly accessorized by a floral-print scarf wrapped gracefully about her neck and secured with a gold brooch. The brim of her brown felt hat was perched just slightly over her left brow. Brown leather pumps and a matching handbag completed the outfit.

Her beautiful appearance totally caught me off guard. Even more, her graceful self-assurance captivated me so much I had to speak to her. "Excuse me, ma'am, but may I compliment you on how very chic and fashionable you look today?"

What that dear lady did next took my very breath away. She placed her right hand on her hip, tossed her head back, and strutted down the store aisle like a high-powered fashion model on a New York runway. After walking a few feet down the aisle, she did a one-eighty-degree turn on her toes and sashayed her way back toward me.

I got in on the game as I picked up my imaginary photographer's camera and exclaimed, "Work it! Work it, girl! The camera loves you!" By the time she strutted back to me, we were both enjoying big belly laughter. We were two total strangers caught up in a beautiful, spontaneous moment of pure delight.

What happened next is etched in my memory. She paused to catch her breath as our laughter subsided. Then she said some words I never expected to hear: "My husband died six months ago. He used to compliment me on my appearance. Since his passing, no one is there to tell me how nice I look. Your compliment is the first one I have had in six months."

My heart sank as I heard her story. I was humbled that this stranger would open up her heart so readily. I looked her in the eye and expressed my heartfelt condolences for the loss of her husband. Then I felt a gentle nudge-like impression I knew was from the Holy Spirit.

"If you don't mind, could I pray for you?" I tenderly asked.

This dear, precious woman, crushed by the pain of loneliness and grief, answered in a broken voice, "Yes, please. Please pray for me. I could use your prayers."

I fought back tears, took her gently by the hand, and prayed a short prayer. I thanked the Lord that He had been her companion and provider and that He was gracious to allow me to meet her. I prayed that God would continue to bless her and remind her that she is loved and always on His heart and mind.

This beautiful woman reached out to me and gave me a hug. As we went our separate ways, I was humbled by the fact that God would use me to be a spark of joy and a beacon of hope. He used my words to encourage her. And He gave me the confidence to speak the right words that resonated with her circumstances. Only God could have orchestrated that moment. Some would call that meeting a coincidence, but I call it providence because I know that the Lord orders the steps of righteous people. I am learning that wherever light is present, burdens are lifted, darkness flees, and everyone gets blessed.

Everywhere you go, the Lord orders your steps. You are on a mission. Yes, a mission from God. If you decide to accept this mission, then you must allow God to put you in the path of hurting people. Go where the people are. When you do, you may come across someone who has a need, and God will ask you to fill that need. Someone will need encouragement. God will ask you to look that person in the eye and smile.

Someone may need prayer. God will nudge you to pray. Someone will need to hear the message of salvation. God will inspire you to share the good news.

I am learning that wherever light is present, burdens are lifted, darkness flees, and everyone gets blessed.

How do you do all of this? Just start. Take a simple step of faith, and be the one to lead the way. Be watchful. Be mindful. Be prayerful. As people meet you, they will take note of how you live your faith out loud.

Remember this little rhyme: "The only Jesus some people will ever see is the Jesus they see in you and in me." When you shine, many people will welcome you and run to your light. Others will be repelled and run from it. How people respond is not your concern. Say yes to God, regardless. He will take care of the rest.

I must share a few words of the song I wrote that inspired this book. "Each One Reach One" is still a mainstay in my concert repertoire after recording it early in my career because it represents my personal desire to share my faith so succinctly. I think this is the perfect time to share it with you. The lyrics remind me of the joy I have when sharing my own faith with others. I'll share the first verse and the chorus as a way to close our discussion on the power of being an evangelist. After reading the lyrics, turn the words into a personal prayer, asking God to help you see yourself as the light He wants you to be.

Today a man is somewhere, proclaiming the Good News
Winning families to Jesus all around the neighborhood
He tells them that God is able
To make their house a home
He wants to win his world for Christ
But he can't do it alone

But, each one can reach one
As we follow after Christ, we all can lead one
We can lead one to the Savior
Then together we can tell the world
That Jesus is the way
If we, each one, reach one[3]

Reflections

1. What does understanding that you are the light of the world mean to you?

2. How can your life be like a city on a hill?

3. How can your life point others to Christ instead of pointing them to you?

4. John 3:19 says that men love darkness rather than light. Why are you tempted to remain in the darkness rather than allow the light of Christ to draw you to Him?

5. How does Christ Jesus empower you to remain in His light?

6. In what ways can you share the beauty of Christ's light with someone who is in need of Him?

Chapter 2

Surrender Your Light

__Let__ your light so shine before men,
that they may see your good works and
glorify your Father in heaven.

Matthew 5:16

Sharing the gospel is a lot like tossing seeds into the wind. Once seeds are sown in good ground, there's no telling how those small kernels will sprout a shoot, take root, and bear fruit. That is the story of some of the most recognized evangelists in history. Even years after their deaths, their influence continues to reap a harvest of souls for the kingdom of God.

Edward Kimball (1823–1901) was a Sunday school teacher who wanted to see every student in his class come to Christ. Knowing that reaching adolescent boys with the gospel message would be a challenge, Kimball endeavored to make a personal appeal to each student in his class. One day, Kimball paid a visit to a local shoe store where one teen worked as a stock boy. Kimball explained the importance of a relationship with Jesus, and his student prayed and gave his heart to Christ in the stockroom. That young man's name was Dwight L. Moody. He began preaching to young men at a local YMCA and went on to win both Protestants and Catholics to

Christ. During his lifetime (1837–1899), D. L. Moody touched two continents with the gospel and established the Moody Bible Institute.[1]

One day while in England, Moody preached a sermon in a small chapel pastored by a young man named Frederick Meyer (1847–1929). Moody's sermon inspired Meyer to become an evangelist. Eventually Meyer preached in America in the town of Northfield, Massachusetts, where a young preacher by the name of John Wilbur Chapman responded to the call of God to become an evangelist.[2]

John Wilbur Chapman (1859–1918) became a persuasive evangelist who preached to thousands in his meetings. One day Chapman was introduced to a former professional baseball player, and he offered to take the young man on as an assistant to his evangelistic efforts. That man was Billy Sunday (1862–1935). After Chapman accepted a call to pastor a church, Billy Sunday began his own preaching ministry, and over time, he preached in some of the nation's largest cities.[3]

One such city was Charlotte, North Carolina. Billy Sunday held evangelistic services there and began a men's fellowship group. That group invited a man named Mordecai Ham (1877–1961) to come and speak. He led more than thirty-three thousand people to the Lord during the first year of his ministry. One November evening in 1934 while Dr. Ham was preaching in Charlotte, a sixteen-year-old boy by the name of Billy Graham (1918–2018) went forward to accept Christ.[4]

Over a period of more than fifty-five years, through live crusades and televised programs, Billy Graham preached the gospel message to more than 210 million people.[5] In October 1986, it was my honor to sing in my first Billy Graham crusade. I sang for the Billy Graham Evangelistic Association in many cities all over the United States and Canada and in Tokyo, Japan. What a sight it was to witness thousands of people empty stadium seats and come forward to give their lives to Christ.

That is an amazing *Each One Reach One* story! There is no telling how God can use hearts and lives that are fully surrendered to Him. There is no way of knowing how your life will influence someone else to come to Christ. By simple faith, we do what we can. God, in His sovereignty, does what we cannot.

Those men surrendered their lives to evangelism. But surrender isn't fashionable. You won't hear the hymn "Just as I Am" on mainstream playlists. Instead, you might hear "Go Your Own Way," "I Won't Back Down," "I Will Survive," and "Me, Myself and I." Surrender is not hip or trendy. No, surrender is hard.

We've been tempted to go our own way ever since we went through the terrible twos. The two-year-old toddler is known for wanting things his way. If he doesn't get what he wants, his disappointment is followed by outbursts of anger, temper tantrums, defiance, and frustration. Does any of that sound familiar? Maybe you've seen that kind of behavior in your own children. Unfortunately, many of us have carried some of the traits of a two-year-old into our adulthood, haven't we? If any of that resonates with you, say "Amen" or "Ouch" right here.

What would it look like if your entire life was completely submitted to the Lord? Would you express unconditional love more easily? Maybe you would witness for Christ more readily. What about personal worship? How would spending more time just enjoying the Lord's presence impact the overall quality of your life? How would this aid you in becoming less resistant to God's instruction and more obedient to His will?

A surrendered life is yielding your power, your will, and your way over to God. Hypothetically speaking, imagine raising the white flag that represents your life, giving up your selfish desires, giving over your personal preferences and prejudices, and giving in to God's will and purpose for your life. You see, the salvation experience is more than accepting Jesus. It's yielding to Him. Surrender is willingly saying yes to God in every area of life. When we lay our agenda down and put God first, He can truly use us to shine for Him.

Let me remind you that your life and your light are synonymous. When you yield your life to God, you are surrendering your light to be a beacon in the dark.

Matthew 6:33 is a landmark passage: "But seek ye first the kingdom of God, and his righteousness; and all these things shall be added unto you" (KJV). I discovered that same powerful message in *The Living Bible* in Proverbs 3:4–6. I suggest you read it thoughtfully and prayerfully, paying close attention to the "if" and "then" statements: "If you want favor with both God and man, and a reputation for good judgment and common sense, then trust the Lord completely; don't ever trust yourself. In everything you do, put God first, and he will direct you and crown your efforts with success." This passage encourages us to surrender *everything* to God for true success in life. Did you notice that the word *everything* is a compound word? Surrendering *every thing* actually means turning over "all that exists."[6] Not just everything as a whole. But each and every individual thing. Each minute detail of your life. Every hope for your future or desire for your family. Your greatest aspirations or your smallest inhibitions. Your diet and exercise plan or recent health challenge. Surrender means asking God for patience to work with difficult people. It means seeking God's will concerning your day-to-day agenda or life's greatest decisions. Surrender means giving all that exists up to God.

One of the greatest lessons I've learned is to let go and let God have His way in my life. He can do much more with my life than I can. That is true for all of us. The journey of surrender is not a one and done, but with every challenge we face, God will revolutionize every area of a life that is submitted to Him.

We discovered in chapter 1 that Matthew 5:14 says *you* are the light. You shine because Jesus shines through you. And verse 16 implies that you must yield the right of way, allowing Him to have full access to the light in order that you can be most effective. What God is looking for is complete surrender.

In all practicality, what does this look like? Personally speaking, in what way could you grant God more access to your light in order to make Him look good to others? Let's explore the answer to those questions more closely.

Let God Have His Way

When Jesus preached to the multitude about the kingdom of light, He commanded His listeners to put their faith into action. Let's study our key verse, Matthew 5:16, closely: "Let your light so shine before men, that they may see your good works and glorify your Father in heaven." We don't have to go too far into the verse before we hear Christ's command. The first command is also the first word: *let*. The meaning of the verb *let* is to allow, permit, make way for, authorize, give permission to, sanction, or admit.[7]

In what way does this verse resonate with you? Have you *let* Jesus have free access to your heart? Surrendering your light, turning your life over to Christ, and giving Him permission to use your life as a light are the first steps. What matters most is living a life that is pleasing to God. Not because you have to, but because you want to live a life that pleases God. It all starts with humility—putting Christ first in all we do.

What does humility have to do with sharing Christ's love? Actually, there is no way to effectively share the gospel without it. The word *humility* means "freedom from pride or arrogance; the quality or state of being humble."[8] We must make the decision to be sympathetic and kindhearted, putting the needs of others before our own.

Humility is not about putting yourself down; it's about putting yourself in the right place. Author and pastor Rick Warren said it like this: "Humility is not thinking less of yourself; it is thinking of yourself less."[9]

If you are genuinely interested in sharing the gospel with the people around you, possessing humility and love for others is where to begin. Philippians 2:3–4 captures this posture: "Do nothing from selfish ambition or conceit, but in humility count others more significant than yourselves. Let each of you look not only to his own interests, but also to the interests of others" (ESV).

On a Mission

Throughout my youth, I observed missionaries—mostly women from our church and the surrounding community—who visited the sick, prayed for those who were in trouble, and tended to the needs of the poor. They did an effective job of reaching out to those in need in our community. However, I never heard stories of African Americans on the foreign mission field. I didn't read the adventures of Black missionaries who went off to faraway places to share the gospel. On television and in Christian magazines, I learned of missionaries who went to remote places such as Zambia or New Guinea. But most of them were white. Many of the stories I read were of single women who didn't have children.

It was no fault of my own, but information concerning Black missionaries was not always available. And in most cases, the resources to publish their stories were not accessible. This lack of information followed me into my adult years. Since I was younger, Black, and married with a family, I concluded that being a missionary and going off to faraway places wasn't something God wanted me to pursue. I just assumed Black people didn't go on the foreign mission field.

It's sad to say, but due to a lack of information, I was wrong about that. In spite of poverty, slavery, and Jim Crow laws, Black missionaries have always found a way to answer God's call to take the gospel message to foreign lands. Black missionaries haven't always been celebrated in books and magazines. Their stories haven't always been the subject of documentaries and motion pictures. But they have always played a leading role in winning people to Christ. The number of Black missionaries is minute compared to their white counterparts. But numbers are growing. In the mid-1980s, I was invited as a guest to sing at a mission conference hosted by African Americans. For the first time in my life, I saw with my own eyes and heard with my own ears the amazing stories of Black missionaries. I was inspired by how God had been and still is using people of color all over the United States and in the uttermost parts of the foreign world.

As a result of that conference, I met and became great friends with a husband-and-wife team, Rich and Jane Berry, who are career missionaries. As Black people on the mission field, trailblazers in the seventies and eighties, and the first Black people to serve with the Navigators mission organization, they have embraced the call to missions as a lifelong endeavor. God used them to open doors, to break down the color barrier, to open minds, and to shatter stereotypes and preconceived notions that God calls only a select group of people as missionaries. They taught me that every believer, regardless of race or culture, is called to the mission field—wherever that takes them. I recently had a conversation with Rich. He emphasized that our passion to reach people for Christ should motivate us to reach people wherever we go. Even if those we meet are different:

> If we just stepped across the street and ministered to neighbors, we would be evangelists. We would be people who were hearing from God to share our faith. But when you interject "mission" and "missionary" into the equation, the understanding is you're going beyond your zip code. You're going beyond your street. And you're going to talk to somebody who is different. We should see ourselves as missionaries who start in our Jerusalem, but be willing to go to Judea, Samaria, and the utmost part of the world.[10]

Rich and Jane Berry have been an inspiration to me in my desire to share Christ. They represent what service and sacrifice look like. They made those attributes appear as highly desirable qualities. Those are qualities I want to emulate. God also used them to increase my love for the church. When I stand onstage and lead the body of Christ in worship, it's a bit like dress rehearsal for heaven. Heaven won't consist of one denomination or race of people. According to Revelation 7:9, every nation, tribe, people, and language will be present in the worship service around God's throne.

**When I stand onstage
and lead the body
of Christ in worship,
it's a bit like dress
rehearsal for heaven.**

Jonah's Mission Trip

There is an Old Testament prophet who knew the Lord's call would demand that he minister to people who were not at all like him. That prophet's name was Jonah. His story is written in the book that bears his name. Short and to the point, this historic narrative is only four chapters long. But it packs a real punch. The whole message of Jonah's book is about surrendering to God so His agenda can be carried out. I encourage you to read the entire book. For now, we'll take a look at the highlights.

> The LORD gave this message to Jonah son of Amittai: "Get up and go to the great city of Nineveh. Announce my judgment against it because I have seen how wicked its people are."
>
> But Jonah got up and went in the opposite direction to get away from the LORD. He went down to the port of Joppa, where he found a ship leaving for Tarshish. He bought a ticket and went on board, hoping to escape from the LORD by sailing to Tarshish.
>
> But the LORD hurled a powerful wind over the sea, causing a violent storm that threatened to break the ship apart. Fearing for their lives, the desperate sailors shouted to their gods for help and threw the cargo overboard to lighten the ship.

But all this time Jonah was sound asleep down in the hold. So the captain went down after him. "How can you sleep at a time like this?" he shouted. "Get up and pray to your god! Maybe he will pay attention to us and spare our lives."

Then the crew cast lots to see which of them had offended the gods and caused the terrible storm. When they did this, the lots identified Jonah as the culprit. "Why has this awful storm come down on us?" they demanded. "Who are you? What is your line of work? What country are you from? What is your nationality?" (Jon. 1:1–8 NLT)

Let's pause here for a moment to process the details. People haven't changed much throughout the history of civilization. Hatred, terrorism, violence, and corruption permeated the culture back then just as they do today. Located in what is now modern-day Iraq, Nineveh was the huge urban center of the Assyrian Empire. The city was known for its power and prestige. The people were immoral, wicked idol worshippers. They were Israel's greatest enemy at the time. God told Jonah to go to Nineveh to prophesy destruction and preach repentance. The last thing Jonah wanted to do was preach repentance to godless idol worshippers who despised him, his people, and his God. That would give them the opportunity to come to know God, to repent and be saved from God's judgment. Jonah wanted nothing to do with that. He had determined to do things his own way. As far as Jonah was concerned, the Ninevites deserved God's judgment. Therefore, he ran in the opposite direction—away from Nineveh. We all know you can run fast, and you can run far, but you can't outrun God.

Let's pick the story back up, starting in verse 9.

Jonah answered, "I am a Hebrew, and I worship the LORD, the God of heaven, who made the sea and the land."

The sailors were terrified when they heard this, for he had already told them he was running away from the LORD. "Oh, why did you do it?" they groaned. And since the storm was getting worse all the time, they asked him, "What should we do to you to stop this storm?"

"Throw me into the sea," Jonah said, "and it will become calm again. I know that this terrible storm is all my fault." (vv. 9–12 NLT)

At Jonah's suggestion, that is exactly what happened. They threw Jonah overboard into the raging sea, and immediately the sea became calm. This display of God's great power persuaded the sailors to worship God. Right there, the sailors gave their lives to God and vowed to serve Him.

Imagine Jonah, being tossed into the violent seas like a rag doll. He was going down to his death when he was swallowed by a great big fish. The Bible doesn't say the fish was a whale, only that it was a whale of a fish. Jonah was inside the fish for three days and three nights where he had plenty of time to ponder and pray.

The Bible says Jonah cried out to God. We know Jonah was inside of the fish. But wouldn't you like to know what was inside of Jonah? I can only imagine what was going on in Jonah's mind. Allow me to take some creative liberty here.

Day One: *Wow! That was a close call, God! I could've been fish bait! Thank You for saving my life!*

Day Two: *God, can we rethink this? I really don't want to go and preach to the Ninevites. They're nothin' but a bunch of godless heathens. What should I do about this? Whew, it smells like rotten fish guts in here!*

Day Three: *Okay! Okay, God, I'll do it! I'll go to Nineveh and preach. Just get me outta this fish's smelly belly!*

The Lord heard Jonah's prayers. After three long days, the great fish spat Jonah out onto the beach. God told Jonah a second time to go to the great city of Nineveh.

The Bible says in Jonah 3:3: "This time Jonah obeyed the LORD's command and went to Nineveh, a city so large that it took three days to see it all" (NLT).

Jonah preached the Word of the Lord, and the entire city, from the greatest to the least, fasted and put on sackcloth and ashes to show repentance to the Lord. The king stepped down from his throne to humble himself before the Lord. Even the animals fasted and drank no water. God's message was preached, and the people of Nineveh were spared God's judgment. Most evangelists are disappointed with their preaching if it doesn't result in a harvest of souls. But Jonah was upset because the harvest of souls was so great. The whole city responded to God's compassion and repented before the Lord.

This small book is packed with several great biblical lessons. Let's explore some of them.

God Is Merciful

Jonah learned that God has mercy and compassion on all people—even people we may not like or care about. There may be someone who has hurt you or wounded you in some way. There may even be entire races of people we do not understand. Because of that, we may fear them or distance ourselves from them. The lesson here is that God's mercy and forgiveness are extended to all people. For the same reason God had mercy on you, He has mercy on all people who cry out to Him. He wants them to surrender their lives and serve Jesus as their Savior.

In the Scriptures, the Lord teaches us to extend mercy. How can we do this? We can seek to understand as well as be understood. We can all work together to tear down walls and build bridges, promoting unity among believers. When you witness gossip, backbiting, or divisive conversations that could harm relationships in the body of Christ, you can serve as a buffer, as one who seeks peace. Remember, we are all on the same side—the Lord's side. We may have come here on different ships, but we're all in the same ship now: fellowship. John 3:17 may well summarize Jonah's spiritual insight. The verse tells us, "For God did not send His Son into the world to condemn the world, but that the world through Him might be saved."

God Does Things His Way

Jonah did not care for God's decision to save the Ninevites. In fact, Jonah was downright angry with God for extending His compassion toward them. Jonah knew that when he preached, they would respond and turn toward God. The lesson here is, God works when He wants and how He wants. It's not our program—it's God's. Our responsibility is to resist pride and humble ourselves before the Lord. Jonah's behavior was the very opposite of humility. He was slow to understand that there is a high cost of low living, which in his case detoured and detained God's purpose for him.

Jonah's story reveals to us that disobedience always delays the best God has for us. We never make progress when we disobey. Instead, we digress, staying longer than we want to stay and paying more than we plan to pay. Jonah shows us how these things can defeat God's purpose.

You Can't Run from God, and You Can't Hide from Him

Deep in our hearts we know that's true because, like Jonah, we've all tried to run and hide from God at one time or another. Jonah attempted to run all the way to Tarshish, but God knew where he was the entire time. Why do we try to escape the presence of God? We may run if we've been hurt by people to the point we find it difficult to trust anyone, including God. Oftentimes, we isolate ourselves to such an extent God has to use extreme measures to reach us. Like Jonah, we may run because we want our own way and we don't want to complete the assignment God has called us to do.

Have you ever tried to run instead of saying, "I'm sorry. Please forgive me"? Maybe you have tried to run from a call upon your life or from a ministry assignment. We can't outrun God. At every point of Jonah's journey, when he tried to escape God's reach—He was there. Maybe Jonah thought God's power extended only as far as the land of Israel, and once he ventured across Israel's boundaries, he could exceed God's grasp. We know, however, God already goes before us. Psalm 139:8 says, "If I go up to heaven, you are there; if I go down to the grave, you are there" (NLT). There is no place where God is not, and He'll be waiting for you when you arrive at the place called surrender.

You Can Shine with Authority

"Shine with authority" may sound like a contradiction of terms. And it can be contradictory unless you desire to humbly submit to the will of Christ and walk in His authority. You see, it's not in your authority that you are sent. You represent God's kingdom everywhere you go. Your life and your light belong to Christ. Shining your light is not something you do. It's who you are.

What do we have authority over? We have authority over the enemy, Satan, and his evil works. He is called a liar and the Father of Lies. By using subtle falsehoods, he wants to prohibit you from sharing the gospel. This author of lies has even developed strategies to keep us from experiencing God's forgiveness and grace or sharing with others. Have you believed some of the following lies the Devil has tried to use against you? As you read the lie from the enemy, the Devil, read the corresponding truth from God's Word.

> **The Lie:** Your story is too shameful. Your life is really messed up. God could never forgive you for the things you've done.
>
> **The Truth:** There is nothing you have done that God will not forgive when you pray and earnestly ask Him. There is always grace for the forgiveness you need. You serve the God of second chances. In fact, He is the God of third chances or as many chances as you need to get it right. First John 1:9 tells us, "If we confess our sins, He is faithful and just to forgive us our sins and to cleanse us from all unrighteousness."

The Lie: You've ignored God for way too long. He has turned His back on you and doesn't want to hear from you.

The Truth: Just as a parent longs to hear from her children, God longs to hear from you. Your heavenly Father loves the sound of your voice. You can talk to God about everything. He hears and understands, and He will give you the answers you need. Read this response from God's Word: "I will instruct you and teach you in the way you should go; I will counsel you with my loving eye on you" (Ps. 32:8 NIV).

The Lie: Keep quiet. No one wants to hear about the things God has done for you. Besides, your salvation story is boring. It isn't important enough to even matter.

The Truth: Make no mistake. The stories of what Jesus has done for you really matter. Has God blessed you? Did He save you? Did He also save your family members? Did He heal you? Provide for you? Whatever the details, your testimony will encourage people who can identify with your story. Psalm 66:16 serves as a tremendous encouragement. Make it your reply. "Come and listen, all you who fear God, and I will tell you what he did for me" (NLT).

The Lie: You're not capable of sharing what God has done for you. You'll never find the right words.

The Truth: God says He will give you the wisdom you need and the right words to share. "It is because of him that you are in Christ Jesus, who has become for us wisdom from God—that is, our righteousness, holiness and redemption. Therefore, as it is written: 'Let the one who boasts boast in the Lord'" (1 Cor. 1:30–31 NIV).

The Lie: You are unlovable. Nobody loves you. Even God doesn't love you.

The Truth: God loves you. You are the reason He sent His Son, Jesus, to die for your sins. Remember John 3:16, the Golden Text of the Bible? "For God so loved the world that He gave His only begotten Son, that whoever believes in him should not perish but have everlasting life." One of the greatest weapons you have against the Devil is believing God's Word. You can take authority over the enemy by resisting him. The Bible says when you do, the Devil will flee (James 4:7).

You Can Shine with Sincerity

What is your story of surrender? Every believer who has given their life to Christ has first surrendered to Him. Remember the prayer I told you about in the introduction? That prayer of surrender has taken Charles and me to continents, countries, and cities all over the world.

I never dreamed saying yes to God would place me onstage to sing before presidents and prisoners, before thousands of women at arenas across North America, before countless races and denominations in North America, before small congregations dotting the countrysides in Europe, or in the remotest jungles of Africa. That prayer has changed my heart and my mind, and it has even inspired many songs I've written and recorded across the years. I'll admit, the first person to be impacted by the songs I write is me. That hasn't always been my story though.

During my college years, the music of the Supremes and Aretha Franklin was calling my name. I had a big dream to record for Motown Records, and Detroit was just a few miles down the road. The music I had played in my father's church seemed good enough for my parents, but I wanted to sing the rhythm-and-blues hits that made the seventies famous. I wanted a life that took me beyond the small platform of my dad's church. I tested the waters by singing in bars and clubs on weekends. The applause was enough to entice me to come back for more. All the while, I was still fulfilling my responsibilities at the church.

Combining the two lifestyles was like trying to mix oil and water. I had too much world for the church and too much church for the world, and I didn't fit in either place. Confused and disoriented, my life was like trying to fit a square peg in a round hole; I tried to make sense of it all. Everyone knew I was a preacher's daughter and a Christian. They even questioned why I was singing in the local bar, hanging out with people who had more impact on me than I had on them. In the meantime, I figured I'd get a teaching degree to give me something to fall back on until my dream materialized.

One fall day during the first semester, I stopped to have lunch in the college snack bar. I ordered a cup of beef vegetable soup. It was served in a white Styrofoam cup along with a white plastic spoon. At first, the soup was piping hot. It tasted really good on such a chilly autumn day. But after a few minutes, the soup began to cool down, and the oily residue from the soup began to stick to the side of the cup, forming a greasy ring around the inside. Orange globules of grease sat on the surface of the soup. When I ate a spoonful, the grease rolled off the plastic spoon, leaving a greasy trail of oily beads. Soon the soup began to make me feel nauseous. Just then, a passage from the book of Revelation came flooding into my mind. (In Revelation 3, there is a letter written to a first-century church at Laodicea. But the words from the passage were so applicable to my own life centuries later, it was as if God was reading my mail.) I didn't have my Bible open, but I knew the Bible verse well. I'd heard my father preach from the text many times.

> I know your deeds, that you are neither cold nor hot. I wish you were either one or the other! So, because you are lukewarm—neither hot nor cold—I am about to spit you out of my mouth. (vv. 15–16 NIV)

Instead of "spit," the New King James Version uses the word "vomit." Got the picture? My compromising lifestyle was making God sick to His stomach. Right there at the lunch table in the snack bar, the Holy Spirit sat down and had lunch with me, convicting me of my compromising ways.

When I was a child, Jesus became my Savior, but as a college student, Jesus became my Lord. I surrendered my life completely to the Lord while holding that white, greasy Styrofoam cup. I gave up my Motown plans and began to seek God's will and purpose for my life. Turning my life completely over to the Lord was the best decision I ever made. He began to lead my life according to His plan for me.

Shining your light is not something you do. It's who you are.

What about you? Have you given your life completely to Christ? (If not, see the "Prayer of Salvation and Memory Verses" chapter at the end of this book.) Jonah's story helps us see that if you are holding anything back from Him, it's compromise. You can't walk with God and run with the Devil. You must not compromise your faithfulness to God for the sake of going your own way. James 4:17 says, "So whoever knows the right thing to do and fails to do it, for him it is sin" (ESV). We learned from Jonah's story that disobedience always has consequences. Just as God promised, there will always be a reward for your faithfulness to Christ. Decide now that no matter what others may do or say, you'll remain faithful to Christ, even when things are difficult.

People often ask if I have a favorite song that I've written and recorded. I don't have a favorite. I love them all for different reasons and for different seasons. However, the

song "With All My Heart" is of particular significance, as it represents my season of surrender. If ever there was a song that I've written that speaks to my desire to completely
submit to God, this is it. Each time I sing it, I make a new commitment to Jesus. I'll
close this chapter with the words I wrote as a heartfelt prayer of surrender. As you read
the lyrics, make the words your own prayer to relinquish your heart and life to God.

———————————

In this quiet place with you
I bow before Your throne
I bear the deepest part of me
To You and You alone
I keep no secrets
For there is no thought
You have not known
I bring my best and all the rest
To You and lay them down

With all my heart
I want to love you, Lord
And live my life
Each day to know You more
All that is in me
Is Yours completely
I'll serve You only
With all my heart[11]

Reflections

1. Considering the power of surrender, what is an area of your life that you believe you should surrender to the Lord?

2. What benefits could you experience upon surrendering your life completely to God?

3. What do you stand to lose by not giving God every area of your life?

4. In what way is surrender difficult for you?

5. Can you recall a time when you decided to do things your way, choosing not to surrender to the Lord? What was the outcome of that decision?

6. Take some time now to sit before the Lord and meditate on Matthew 5:16. Ask the Holy Spirit to speak to your heart about how to let your light shine for Him. Allowing the Holy Spirit to guide your thoughts, write down what He is speaking to you.

Chapter 3

Own Your Light

*Let **your light** so shine before men, that they may see your good works and glorify your Father in heaven.*

Matthew 5:16

As a former middle-high school music and English teacher, I know a good teacher is one-fourth instructor and three-fourths actor. Teaching middle school kids is a lot like herding cats. You've got to think fast and be quick on your feet. I was fortunate to have wonderful teachers who inspired my love for the classroom and reinforced my love for music. My first-grade teacher, Mrs. Lillian Melvin, was a great encouragement to me. Our first-grade classroom was directly across the hall from the school's front office. Occasionally, Mrs. Melvin would have to make a quick run to the office to take care of emerging matters. Leaving twenty-five or so rambunctious first graders in a classroom without supervision, even for a few minutes, is a disaster waiting to happen.

Mrs. Melvin was a gifted teacher who always had a backup plan. Before she left the classroom, she would instruct me to sit down at the big upright piano that was in our classroom and lead my classmates in our favorite nursery rhymes until she returned. I would sit at the piano and lead them in a few choruses of "Old MacDonald Had a

Farm," "Twinkle, Twinkle, Little Star," or "Mary Had a Little Lamb." If my repertoire of nursery rhymes ran short, I would strike up a song I knew from church and
turn the entire first-grade class into a gospel choir.

About twenty years later, I was invited to sing at a meeting for a local Christian
women's organization in my hometown. Much to my surprise, Mrs. Melvin was the
president. Because I wanted to serve with her, I quickly volunteered to be the worship leader for the monthly meetings. As Mrs. Melvin grew older and moved into an
assisted-living facility, we enjoyed occasional visits where we would sip tea and talk
about the Lord. Gleaning from her faith was like drinking from a deep well. It didn't
matter that I was an adult; she was always my teacher, and I, her student.

Max Lucado, a bestselling author and pastor, wrote, "To call yourself a child of
God is one thing. To be called a child of God by those who watch your life is another
thing altogether."[1] Certainly Mrs. Melvin was one of God's choicest servants. Even as
a child, I could see the love of God in her life. Every Christ follower is called to live in
such a radically different way that any person who meets them can see their life and
catch a glimpse of God.

A close friend named Yvonne Carey lives in such a way. As a middle school math
coach, she works closely with students and teachers in an inner-city public school in
Michigan. Ms. Carey is a woman of deep and abiding faith in God. She doesn't step
up on a soapbox to broadcast her testimony. She doesn't need to. She lives out her faith
in Christ in everyday ways that make an eternal difference.

There is no way those around Ms. Carey can deny the light she shines. During her
fourteen-year tenure at the school, she has gained a reputation for being a blessing to
her students and colleagues. Every day, she greets them with a warm smile. She stores
snacks in her office cabinet to share with students who haven't had a nourishing meal
that day. Tucked away on another shelf of the same cabinet, she keeps a surplus of
pocket-sized devotional books to share with other teachers who may need an extra
dose of hope.

Sometimes tension can rise on the school campus. The stress of living in single-parent homes, disagreements between students, occasional incidences of violent behavior, disgruntled parents, or troubles at home can wear on students, teachers, and families. When they do, Ms. Carey de-escalates situations with her keen people skills. She shows concern for the families of both students and faculty members. When others seek her counsel, she offers wise, godly advice along with a warm smile and an understanding heart. When a fellow faculty member has a heavy heart upon the passing of a loved one or is facing a difficult challenge in their marriage, they know Ms. Carey has an open-door policy and they are always welcome to step inside her office to find a refuge from life's storms. It's not uncommon for those who seek her out to ask for her prayers. During those moments of confidentiality, no one is the least bit concerned that the government took prayer out of public schools more than sixty years ago.

In the quietness of her office, Ms. Carey stands in the gap and prays for her colleagues and students. Being a blessing comes easily for her. She said it this way: "I try not to look past students and colleagues when seeing them in the classroom or hallways, but with intention and purpose, connect with them, encourage them, and, yes, even pray for them. I want them to know they matter to me and, more important, they matter to God." Yvonne Carey knows if you shine your light, people will find their way to it.

That's why people always found their way to Jesus. He didn't look past them; He acknowledged them. Even more, He loved each person as if they were the only one to love. In John 8:12, we find this amazing declaration: "When Jesus spoke again to the people, he said, 'I am the light of the world. Whoever follows me will never walk in darkness, but will have the light of life'" (NIV). Then Jesus, the light of the world, gave His light to you.

You're not to dismiss this light or take it for granted. God gave you His light for a specific purpose. The light is not to be hidden or put away because of shame, embarrassment, or fear. Think about all God has done for you and let thankfulness fill your heart, for out of the overflow of all you are, your light shines. Put your light high on a lampstand to show the way for people you encounter, first at home and then everywhere you go.

When we built our home a few years ago, each light fixture and electrical outlet was intentionally placed as a part of our home's design. There was nothing haphazard about it. Everything about the process was planned with great intention so we could enjoy the form and the function of lighting in our home. In the same way, the light God has given you should be acknowledged as coming from Him. You should treat your light as a gift from God to be used for the purpose of glorifying Him. To be most effective in your realm of influence, you must own your light, maintain the light, and then do everything you can to keep the light from growing dim.

How do you do that? Matthew 5:16 says, "Let *your light* so shine before men ..." In the same way your front porch light welcomes visitors to your home, your light should always be on, inviting those you encounter to experience the light of Christ in you.

Think about the many functions a light has. A beam of light can dispel darkness on the road the way an automobile's headlight does. Light illuminates the way just as light shines on a darkened path. Lights can brighten up an entire city block the way Times Square lights up the streets of New York City. Light adds beauty and design in the same way that a lovely chandelier adds elegance to a hotel lobby. Light can create a certain mood the way candles make a dining experience special during a romantic dinner. Photographers place their subjects in the highest quality light possible for the best images. Lights can add security and deter crimes in mall parking lots. Like a neon sign, light can bring attention to a special attraction.

Now, think about how shining with intention can increase the impact of *your* light. Christ commands us to be a light to the people around us. This is possible only when you encounter people, establishing connections and interactions. In this chapter, I want to talk about how important it is to shine your light with confidence and purpose, taking thought to how you can have the strongest effect on others. You are to take the mission personally. But first, I want to share an encounter that taught me a great lesson about owning my light.

Piggly Wiggly Prayer Meeting

One day, I was standing in the checkout lane at the local Piggly Wiggly grocery store. (Yes. The Piggly Wiggly is not just a grocery store featured in movies about the South. That's the name of a real chain of grocery stores. We have a Piggly Wiggly in the small Georgia farm community where we live.) I was waiting my turn to pay for my groceries when a familiar song on the store's sound system caught my ear. Not one to miss an opportunity to encourage myself, I softly hummed along. I was careful not to intrude on the space of the gentleman ahead of me who was already being waited on by the clerk, but he must have overheard me anyway.

He turned to me and said politely, "Hey! That sounds pretty good. You should sing for a living!"

I chuckled softly and responded, "Well, I do sing for a living!"

"Well, sing something for me right now!"

Without a moment's hesitation, I eased my shopping cart forward a little and sang at a volume I thought he could appreciate. I was careful not to distract others around me. I started in on the familiar hymn. "Amazing grace! How sweet the sound ..."

All of a sudden, the volume of the store's sound system went mute, and a young man I assumed was the manager came out of his office cubbyhole at the front of the store. He stood at the foot of the checkout, lifted his hands toward the heavens, closed his eyes, and worshipped. In seconds, a small crowd of onlookers gathered with him around the checkout lane.

When I saw I had an audience, I turned up the volume and sang with more intention. Actually, I added a few nuances, the way I would sing the song if I had been back home at my father's Black Baptist church. I continued, "That saved a wretch like me! I once was lost, but now am found, was blind, but now I see."

More people stopped to listen, so I continued to sing. "When we've been there ten thousand years, bright shining as the sun, we've no less days to sing God's praise than when we'd first begun."[2] After I finished singing the hymn, the gentleman ahead of me smiled with delight as he joined in applauding with the crowd. The store manager said a hearty "Amen" before he went back to work, and a few folks joined him as they left the store or went back to their shopping. The gentleman smiled and thanked me for the song as he grabbed his grocery bags and headed toward the exit. I pushed my cart up and put my items on the conveyor belt.

The clerk appeared to be around twenty years old. As she scanned my grocery items, she started a conversation. "'Amazing Grace.' I love that song. That is my grandmother's favorite hymn. She's not doing so well right now. She's at home fighting cancer."

"I am so sorry to hear that your grandmother is ill," I replied with empathy; then I asked how her grandmother was progressing in her cancer battle.

"She has good days and bad days."

"Do you mind if I pray for your grandmother?" I asked.

The young lady immediately stopped checking my groceries and stood perfectly still, waiting for me to pray. After moving a few steps closer to her, I bowed my head. My prayer was simple and conversational. I wanted her to understand that prayer is simply having a heartfelt talk with a holy God. You can stop and talk to God at any moment. There was a confident sense of knowing God was hearing our prayer as we asked Him to heal the young lady's grandmother. She listened with her eyes closed as I thanked God for her courage to tell me of her grandmother's plight. "Lord, give her courage and boldness to live her life as a witness for Christ in front of her young peers," I ended the prayer. She said "Amen" with me.

Afterward, I encouraged her to be faithful to God and continue to advocate for her aging grandmother. I paid for my groceries, bid her a "God bless you," and was headed for the exit when a dear lady stopped me and asked me to pray for her husband, who was not serving the Lord. After I prayed with her, I made my way to my car where another woman met me in the parking lot. She identified herself as a single mother and asked me to pray for her and her small children.

It was evident that day in the Piggly Wiggly that the people there needed the Lord. It was also obvious to me that everywhere I go, there are people in my path who are desperate for Jesus to shine on their circumstances. Some of them are dangling by a thread, so to speak. Others are facing gigantic mountains. With just a few words of encouragement, I could be a lifeline. Here's what I learned that day: Shining the light for Christ is not a random act. It's an intentional response to the needs of others.

Prayer is simply having a heartfelt talk with a holy God.

Maybe you have been a recipient of someone's generosity, thoughtfulness, or show of empathy. Has anyone ever encouraged you with just the right words, seemingly when you needed it most? Perhaps someone has surprised you by paying for your meal when you ate out or treated you to a cup of specialty coffee. Maybe a stranger held the door open for you or helped you get your groceries in or out of your vehicle. Possibly someone remembered your birthday when you thought everyone had forgotten. Kindness can mean being friendly, giving generously, or showing empathy. You don't have to give an impromptu concert at Piggly Wiggly. But within your sphere of influence, wherever that leads, you can be ready to meet a need when God brings the opportunity to you.

People call these bright spots in our lives "random acts of kindness," meaning, they just happen here and there. Kindness really shouldn't be considered a random act. The Bible identifies kindness as a spiritual virtue, one that needs cultivation just like faith and patience. Let's look at the role kindness plays in winning others to Jesus.

Kindness—Sow It Generously

Not long ago, Charles and I flew back home to Atlanta after a weekend engagement. Once we arrived in the airport baggage claim area, Charles left to get the larger pieces of luggage. As I stood waiting, a skycap with the kindest face and most gentle demeanor approached me and asked if I needed his help. I smiled and told him no, thanking him for asking. As he turned, he spoke the words, "All right then. Have a nice day. God bless you."

I stopped him and said, "That's the reason why you are so kind. Isn't it?" He seemed puzzled. I said, "You are so kind because you know the Lord. Don't you?" The young man's face beamed like a light bulb as he acknowledged that he did know the Lord. Then he pulled out his cell phone and showed me an app that featured the Scripture from Galatians 5:22–23 about the fruit of the Spirit. He even shared some of his thoughts on kindness. We talked about the Lord, and I commended him for being a student of God's Word. I encouraged him to continue spreading kindness. It was obvious that the airport was the perfect mission field for this young man.

Kindness doesn't cost very much, yet it has endless worth and long-lasting value. A kind word or act can heal a broken heart, lift a wounded spirit in an instant, or put a smile on the face of a stranger. The reason? Kindness is not a trivial act. It is the act of being good to another person without reciprocation. According to the Bible, kindness is a fruit of the Spirit that we should practice daily. Galatians 5:22–23 tells us, "The fruit of the Spirit is love, joy, peace, patience, kindness, goodness, faithfulness, gentleness, self-control; against such things there is no law" (ESV). Did you catch that? There is nothing prohibiting us from being kind. There are no biblical or judicial laws against it. Rather, the more kindness the better. Therefore, we should practice it freely and liberally. This virtue distinguishes believers from the rest of the world.

But anybody can be kind. Right? So, what's the difference between being polite and the brand of kindness Christians practice? Consider the source—as a fruit of the Spirit, this supernatural virtue (and every fruit of the Spirit) originates with the heart of God. The kindness you sow has eternal impact. Kindness is powerful. It's like giving hope away to those who feel they are hopeless and all alone in this world.

Ever heard the phrase "kindness is contagious"? The world can often be a harsh, cold, and unfriendly place. People can choose to go through their day with a bad attitude, sowing discord and treating people with disrespect. If you are not careful, that kind of attitude can rub off and ruin your entire day. Then you may pass on that sour attitude to others in your sphere of influence. A bad attitude can have a trickle-down effect.

Instead, God's Word encourages us to choose kindness as a lifestyle. Let kindness define the way you live. When you are good to someone, that person benefits from your kind words or your benevolent act, and in turn, they have a good chance of paying it forward, extending a kindness to someone in their world. That way, people are more likely to "catch kindness" from you and give it away to someone else later. When we get ready for work or church, we dress ourselves to look our best. We shower, put on a nice outfit with some coordinating accessories. We fix our hair and maybe put on some makeup to enhance our features. The process requires our full attention and our best intentions.

Just as you would put on your favorite pair of shoes, the Bible says to put on kindness. Picture the intentional practice of sitting down, slipping on your shoes, and lacing them up before you go out the door at the start of your day. Colossians 3:12 tells us to go through a similar spiritual process. It says, "Put on then, as God's chosen ones, holy and beloved, compassionate hearts, kindness, humility, meekness, and patience" (ESV). Genuine kindness accompanies all the fruit of the Spirit. When you put on kindness, you're dressing yourself in love, joy, peace, patience, and all the other attributes of the Spirit of God. Have you ever chosen to wear your favorite color because it complements the color of your hair? In the same way, clothe yourself in kindness so it covers and even complements you in all you do. By putting on Christ, the power of His love transforms you, making you ready for His holy purposes.

In other words, when sowing kindness, be generous. Generosity has its benefits. Have you ever noticed that kindness has a way of disarming people? They feel seen and affirmed. They feel less threatened and defensive. When we hear a story of someone who has performed a meaningful act of kindness, it motivates us to do the same. It's proven to be true. If you make the effort to bless someone, you're likely to get a blessing in return. Isn't that what the Bible says? "Give, and you will receive. Your gift will return to you in full—pressed down, shaken together to make room for more, running over, and poured into your lap. The amount you give will determine the amount you get back" (Luke 6:38 NLT).

Kindness is not a trivial act. It is the act of being good to another person without reciprocation.

Kindness—Use It Intentionally

Kindness is good for the marriage relationship. A crucial element for emotional bonding and good communication, kindness heightens trust, nurtures interaction, aids in conflict resolution, and creates a feeling of safety and security. Married couples can appreciate it when a spouse goes out of their way to be helpful and supportive. Kind acts are like thousands of threads that bind a couple together in love. Research shows that the ingredient that is most often missing in failed marriages but is common in successful ones is kindness. Married couples who are generous with kindness are more likely to find a deeper sense of satisfaction and stability in their marriage relationship. Practicing kindness makes couples feel cared for, validated, understood, and most of all, loved.[3] It sounds simple, yet it's quite profound. Kindness is the glue that holds marriages together.

Kindness is good for the workplace. It increases employee performance and morale.[4] Business professionals even use kindness as a strategy for success because a salesperson who is kind to his customers and clients makes more sales, which is good for the company's bottom line. According to the *Harvard Business Review*, "If you're an emerging leader, being kind to your employees can help you retain top talent, establish a thriving culture, increase employee engagement, and enhance productivity."[5] Recent studies show that happy employees not only create a more positive work environment, they contribute to a company's financial success. The bottom line is, happy employees increase company revenue.[6]

In fact, practicing kindness has even proven to have health benefits. When you are kind to someone, your brain releases the feel-good hormone called oxytocin.[7] Performing acts of kindness can lower stress and produce a greater sense of well-being.[8] When you wave at your neighbor with a smile, more than likely, she'll smile and wave back. The virtue of kindness is hugely reciprocal.

There are countless reasons to be kind to others. But the main reason is because that is what Jesus did. And we want to model His life in every way. We want to love as He loved and be good to others, just as He was. Acts 10:38 sums it up beautifully: "God anointed Jesus of Nazareth with the Holy Spirit and with power, who went about doing good and healing all who were oppressed by the devil, for God was with Him."

Kindness—Share It Thoughtfully

Have you ever stopped to take note of how kind Jesus was to those He met during His earthly ministry? He took time to play with children (Matt. 19:14). He looked after widows (Luke 7:11–17). He fed the hungry (John 6:1–15). He cared for the poor (Luke 14:12–14). He healed those with disabilities (Matt. 4:23). He dined with those who were socially unacceptable (Mark 2:15). In other words, Jesus looked for opportunities to be kind to others. He found great joy in giving Himself away for the sake of others.

If we were honest with ourselves, we'd admit that it's not in our nature to be kind. We often think of kindness as a weakness. We think that if we're kind to others, they will take advantage of us. So we tend to guard ourselves, distance ourselves, and even withhold kindness so we don't get hurt. For that reason, kindness doesn't always flow generously because it's not always returned. But kindness is humbly extending ourselves to others even though they may not be able to repay us. Sometimes they don't deserve it, and they may not even thank you.

But don't let that deter you. Yes, you may sow kindness to a particular person, but ultimately, you are honoring Jesus. When you realize that God gave you what you don't deserve—the gift of His own Son—you are reminded to look for opportunities to sow kindness and to do it thoughtfully in the name of Christ.

My family and I received kindness one Sunday after church. We stopped for dinner at one of our favorite restaurants. When it was time for the server to bring the check for our food, she informed us that someone in the restaurant wanted to bless us. They had paid for our meal. Overwhelmed that an unidentified benefactor had decided to bless us in such a generous way, we blessed our server with the same amount that we would have spent on our meal. This was a way to thank her for her service and share the love of Christ with her. I hope that in some way she felt that she was included in passing the blessing around. As a family, we found that any way you look at it, when you sow kindness, everyone gets a blessing. Most of all, the person who gets the biggest blessing is you.

Kindness—Spread It Hopefully

John 8 spotlights a wonderful story about kindness and compassion. Early one morning, Jesus was teaching in the temple when the scribes and Pharisees came to Him. These learned, powerful men were always following Jesus, but not because they believed He was God and wanted to learn from His teaching. Instead, these teachers of the law would contend with Jesus, questioning Him to trap Him so they could accuse Him of blasphemy and kill Him. Their efforts were in vain. In His typical fashion, Jesus presented a wisdom that was too much for them.

On this day, while Jesus was teaching, the scribes and Pharisees dragged in a woman and threw her into the crowd. They said that she had been caught in the very act of sleeping with a man who was not her husband. With pious and religious attitudes, they said, "Now Moses, in the law, commanded us that such should be stoned. But what do You say?" (v. 5).

Jesus didn't say one word. He did something no one expected. As though He didn't even hear them, He stooped down and wrote in the dirt. Scripture doesn't say what He wrote. Perhaps it was one of the Ten Commandments. Since Jesus knew the covert thoughts of every man standing there, maybe He wrote a list of their secret sins in those telling moments. Knowing that adultery is never a solo act, perhaps Jesus wrote the name of her male counterpart, who was conveniently absent from this mock trial. The more questions they hurled at Jesus, the more He wrote. Eventually, Jesus stood up and said, "Let him who is without sin among you be the first to throw a stone at her" (v. 7 ESV).

Jesus stooped back down and continued to write in the dirt. One by one, her accusers turned, dropped their stones, and walked away. When all her accusers were gone, Jesus stood up and saw no one but the woman. "He said to her, 'Woman, where are those accusers of yours? Has no one condemned you?' She said, 'No one, Lord.' And Jesus said to her, 'Neither do I condemn you; go and sin no more'" (vv. 10–11).

Press pause right here. Did you recognize kindness when it quietly stepped into the spotlight? No doubt about it, the woman was guilty of an offense worthy of stoning. She knew it. Jesus knew she was guilty too. He could have said, "You've lived this kind of life for way too long. When are you going to shape up? You know better than to behave in such a disgraceful way. Shame on you!" But from a place of tenderhearted kindness and deep compassion, Jesus offered her forgiveness. No judgment. No finger-pointing. No blaming. By His compassionate behavior, Jesus was basically saying, "You are forgiven. Not shame *on* you. But shame *off* you. You are free of the guilt from your past life. Live with the hope that your best days are still ahead of you." She left with another opportunity to do something valuable and virtuous with her life.

By no means did He excuse her sin. He commanded her to come up higher. No more looking for love in all the wrong places, living beneath her privilege. In the same compassionate breath, Jesus brought her sin to the light and gave her a second chance at living. "Go and sin no more." This adulteress met the Light of the World, and she would be different from that day forward. Think about that for just a moment. "The wages of sin is death," according to Romans 6:23. Your sins and mine are more than enough to earn us the death penalty. But Jesus offers us enough kindness, compassion, and forgiveness to last us an eternity. Jesus came not just to tell us what kindness is. He demonstrated its power in flesh and blood.

Five Simple Rules of Kindness

Have you noticed that it's easy to brush people off from a distance? Often when we don't know a person's pain or the details of their circumstances, we tend to be short and impatient with them. But once we slow down and look at their situation more closely, our opinion of them will likely change. For those you love or for strangers you meet along the way, remember that kindness is not random but a daily practice.

Here are five simple rules of kindness. With every opportunity, we should walk them out.

Rule 1: Have a Heart

Everybody you encounter along the way is struggling in a battle you know nothing about. People are typically in a storm, coming out of a storm, or headed for another storm. Be kind. Be the refuge they need. When you practice empathy or try to have a better understanding of the difficulties people are facing, you will find people letting down their guard and opening their hearts. They become vulnerable and even transparent. When you hear the details of their story, have compassion for them. Underneath the surface is a heart that has been wounded by pain or tragedy. Do your best to sympathize with them, as described in 1 Peter 3:8: "All of you, be like-minded, be sympathetic, love one another, be compassionate and humble" (NIV).

Rule 2: Lend a Hand

When you lift up others, you are emulating the qualities and the actions of Jesus Christ, reflecting His love and teachings. I learned one day that everybody needs kindness in a deeply profound way. I had the opportunity to sing for the Cobb County Prayer Breakfast, an annual event held in north Atlanta on the National Day of Prayer. Diplomat, civil rights activist, and former Atlanta mayor, Andrew Young—a man then in his eighties—was the event's speaker. We were both scheduled for early morning sound checks, so we arrived at the venue at about the same time. After our sound checks, I noticed that this great man was sitting alone at a table nearby. The doors to the meeting room were still closed, and the room was quiet, so I took the opportunity to ask him for a photograph. He said graciously, "I'd be happy to, but you'll need to give me a hand to lift me up from my chair."

I replied with a smile, "Ambassador Young, you've been lifting up people around the world for decades. It would be my honor to return the favor." What a privilege it was to extend a hand to someone who has extended kindness to people across the globe and devoted his life to advocating for others.

Jesus teaches us that when we practice kindness by lifting up others, our backs get stronger, and our shoulders get broader. Our Savior was a source of encouragement and affirmation to everyone around Him. With healing and hope, Jesus lifted people's spirits and restored their sense of worth. Similarly, when we lift up others, we affirm their value and potential. We provide the support and encouragement they need to overcome the challenges they may be facing. Most of all, when you practice kindness, you are representing Jesus. *Practice* is the operative word here. Like any skill, the more you practice kindness, the better you will become at it. The results of your kindness will motivate you to continue the habit. And, if your friends lift you up in return, then you are doubly blessed.

Rule 3: Find the Courage

Let's face it. Showing kindness often means stepping out of your comfort zone. Having courage means that you have to face your fears.

Not a people person?

Afraid to take risks?

Not sure of what to say?

Sometimes we don't want to be kind because it may not always be convenient, or we may not feel equipped to meet the need. Sometimes we are too concerned about what others may think of us. Instead of opting for what you *can't* do, default to what you *can* do. Remember, little is much when God is in it. He's the Great Multiplier. He expects us to do what we can do. We can push past the boundaries of our comfort zone to do the right thing. God is always behind the scenes, blessing our efforts, doing above and beyond what we are able to do. Being kind always sets you up for success. Eventually, kindness not only heals others—it heals you.

Rule 4: Let It Go

So many people are easily bothered. When they are slighted or inconvenienced in the least way, sometimes their tempers flare and their words fly. You've heard the saying, "Sticks and stones may break my bones, but words will never hurt me." The words sound good, but they are far from true. Words can hurt! When someone speaks harsh words in anger and haste, things don't usually end well but escalate. Uncontrolled anger only masks a deeper problem of hurt and woundedness.

When you identify these angry episodes in yourself or others, it's the perfect time to be the bigger person and acquiesce. Keep a toehold from becoming a foothold. Don't allow a foothold to become a stronghold. Guard your heart and your mouth by not allowing a stronghold to lead to a stranglehold. In other words, don't allow harsh words to ruin relationships or injure the heart of someone you love. You must not become entangled with such petty things. Just let it go. The Bible calls this attribute *self-control*. This fruit of the Spirit compels you to think before you speak, using your words to build up and not tear down.

The words that come out of our mouths are only an indication of what is in our hearts. When speech is characterized by anger and haste, the fallout can be detrimental. Let's determine in our hearts that the words we speak will bring healing, forgiveness, and encouragement. Words spoken in kindness are words you will never regret saying. "Let no corrupt word proceed out of your mouth," admonishes Ephesians 4:29, "but what is good for necessary edification, that it may impart grace to the hearers."

Rule 5: Count to Five

These five short sentences filled with kind words are the foundation for kindness as a habit. The first sentence consists of one word. The second of two words. The third of three words, and so on. The phrases are easy to remember.

1. Please.
2. Thank you.
3. I love you.
4. Will you forgive me?
5. How may I help you?

Showing Others the Love of God

We talked about the power of kindness early on, but I want to mention another aspect of kindness. During encounters with strangers and friends alike, I have found that the hearts of others open up to kindness and sensitivity as a flower opens to the sun. When people respond to kindness, they may share personal details that otherwise would remain hidden. But on the heels of kindness, a crucial time materializes that can transform into a holy moment. That divine moment is called a *kairos* moment. It's when God invites us to cooperate with the Holy Spirit to do a specific work He wants to accomplish in the world. The word *kairos* derives from an ancient Greek term that is translated as "a fitting season" or "occasion"; "the right/appointed time"; a "special" or "chosen time."[9]

Another phrase to describe a *kairos* moment is "an opportune or seasonable time."[10] You may sense the Holy Spirit's help in a particular situation. He may guide you to speak a word of encouragement to someone in that moment. Or when you speak to someone about the Lord, they receive the words with faith and obedience. When you sense these elements, you are experiencing a *kairos* moment. The stories that I share in this book are those divine appointments when I knew God was present in each of those moments, using me to accomplish His purposes.

As you take the time to help others, you'll begin to recognize these special moments when God, in His undeniable presence, walks right into the situation to answer a present need. This is always an unmistakable moment when the Holy Spirit senses He is welcome in your situation to assist you in serving others.

Whenever the Holy Spirit makes His presence known, shining our lights becomes easy because He assists us in sharing His love with others. As we walk with God— paying close attention to the Holy Spirit's nudges—we can learn to recognize those moments when they occur.

You may think those moments are rare, but I have learned that the Holy Spirit is continually working, creating these moments to partner with us. He is only waiting for someone who will yield themselves in obedience. Your part is to yield yourself and step into the moment by obeying the Holy Spirit's guidance.

I have taken an inventory of the people I've met and the conversations I've had with them about the Lord. Most of the time, the encounter was initiated by a need on their part and an act of kindness on my part. With the Holy Spirit's help, I was able to engage with a person in that moment. When I say "engage with a person," I mean I was able to see them through the eyes of kindness. I'm not talking about a glance or a brief notice in passing. Everyone you meet has value and deserves validation as a part of God's creation. Something beautiful happens when we pause long enough to acknowledge people, recognizing each one as someone who is loved by God—as someone for whom Jesus died.

As you listen with your heart in that moment, the Holy Spirit will aid you to sense the other person's need. People can build up defensive walls around their hearts. But kindness can tear walls down in an instant. You don't want to miss that moment when it happens. That person who is suffering is often silently praying deep inside for someone to show them the hope they long for. I heard that cry when the two women in the checkout lane and the young clerk at Sam's Club all asked for a blessing.

I sensed that subtle cry for help when the widow in the department store said, "My husband died six months ago."

I perceived that the gentleman in the checkout lane at the Piggly Wiggly was reaching out for hope when he said to me, "Sing a song for me right now."

Wherever the need is, Jesus is there to meet it. Don't miss that critical moment! That's when you can be the answer to someone's prayer. Could I lead you in a prayer now, that you will see those God moments and seize them when they come your way?

Dear God, thank You for the light You have given me. Help me to understand that I could be the answer to a prayer someone is praying even now. I don't want to miss You or the opportunity to shine my light for You. Thank You, Lord. In Christ's name, amen.

Reflections

1. After reading the chapter, spend some time in personal reflection and ask yourself, "Am I really as kind as I think I am or is there room for me to grow in this area?"

2. Why does kindness matter?

3. What is one thing you can do today that will challenge you to be kinder?

4. Who are the kindest people you know? What can you learn from them?

5. What is one of the kindest things someone has ever done for you? What impact did it have on your life?

6. In the encounter between Jesus and the woman caught in the act of adultery, what difference did Jesus' kindness have on her life? How might she have paid kindness forward?

7. Think of a time you experienced or witnessed a *kairos* moment either in real life or through a story. What was that moment like? How can you be more sensitive so you can recognize those moments in the future?

8. What personal barriers hinder you from being kind? Fear? Low self-esteem? Shame? Hurt or woundedness? What would happen if you presented those barriers to Jesus now and exchanged those hindrances for a heart of kindness?

Chapter 4

Turn Up Your Light

*Let your light **so shine** before men, that they may see your*
good works and glorify your Father in heaven.

Matthew 5:16

Reading the fascinating stories of missionaries and the exciting adventures they experienced has a way of deepening our faith and inspiring us to partner with God, wherever that takes us. I have always admired the courage and obedience of missionaries who heard the call of God, left all the things that were familiar or comfortable, and went off to serve God on the mission field. The term "on the mission field" connotes adventure, mystery, and discovery. The mission field may be across the globe or across the tracks. Either way, adventure awaits. Some missionaries serve God as preachers, teachers, day care workers, or Bible translators. Still others put their very lives on the line and make the ultimate sacrifice. The lives of Elisabeth and Jim Elliot are all that rolled into one unforgettable story.[1]

Elisabeth and Jim Elliot were committed to a life of evangelism in the most profound way. The impact they made for the sake of the gospel continues to be a powerful catalyst today. In 1956, Jim had a deep desire to evangelize the Waodani tribe (then known as the Auca), an indigenous people group in the Amazon forest of eastern

Ecuador.[2] This tribe was known for their savage way of living and their resistance to outsiders. Fortified by a relentless call from God, Jim and four other missionary companions landed their small aircraft on a sandbar in a remote part of the jungle occupied by the Waodani. Through demonstrations of kindness and simple gifts of buttons and rock salt, the team of young missionaries seemed to be making progress and gaining the trust of the Waodani tribe. The missionaries even used a loudspeaker to shout simple phrases in the tribe's native language. The Waodani tribe members reciprocated, exchanging gifts of their own.

One day, without warning, native warriors from the tribe appeared from out of the jungle armed with spears. Jim Elliot, Nate Saint, Roger Youderian, Ed McCully, and Pete Fleming were brutally attacked and massacred that day. The oldest, Nate Saint, was only thirty-two years old.[3]

Even after this tragic event, Elisabeth and other missionaries returned to the Waodani people, where they continued their evangelistic efforts. The Elliots and their companions made tremendous sacrifices that motivated an explosion in the missionary movement around the world.[4] Jim and Elisabeth Elliot, and others like them, are a testament to the high cost of following Jesus.

You may not be called to go on a mission to the Amazon jungles of South America, but you must be willing to put Christ first in everything you do and obey the call He has on your life. In our relationship with Christ, it is all, or it is nothing at all. Over and over, the Bible reminds us that it costs much to be a believer in Christ Jesus. Consider how the following passage applies to your life. Luke 9:23 says, "If anyone desires to come after Me, let him deny himself, and take up his cross daily, and follow Me."

If you and I really believe the gospel is true, then we will be moved to do everything we can with everything we have to reach people with the gospel. The world around us is growing darker with each day. Shining His light is one way to share that lifesaving message with the world.

You don't have to go very far to find someone who is lost without Christ, hurting from loneliness, a victim of hunger, or suffering from sickness and disease. People and pain are constant companions. Because shining the light is all about introducing people to the saving power of Jesus, we should have a sense of urgency, motivated by the love of God, to do everything within our power to bring people to Him.

Hold High the Light

When you are willing to be a witness for Christ, you'll find that opportunities to be a light for Him are constantly available. With the help of the Holy Spirit who leads and guides us, we can become more sensitive to the needs of others around us.

That is what happened one evening when I was invited to attend the monthly meeting of a local songwriter's group in the Atlanta area. The group's president had given me the address where the group would meet. I invited a couple of friends to join me, and we rode together. Headed for an unfamiliar area of town, we followed the GPS instructions carefully. After a forty-five-minute drive, I was a bit taken aback when we arrived at the parking lot of a corner bar.

My friends and I chuckled at the prospect of hanging out at the bar for the evening. We had a quick prayer meeting in the car, asking God to help us represent Him well. Once inside, we settled at a table.

The group's president, whom we'll call Joe, was already onstage jamming with the band. He saw that I had arrived, and a few minutes later, he called me up to the stage to join them in a spontaneous jam session. I greeted the crowd and said to Joe, "Hey, let's do 'Amazing Grace' in the key of C." With a gospel flair, we sang a few verses of the favorite hymn.

After we finished, someone from the back of the room shouted, "Sing another one!" So I said to the band, "Let's do 'Just a Closer Walk with Thee,' Louisiana blues style." When we were done, someone shouted, "Sing 'How Great Thou Art.'" After that, there was another request to sing "Shout to the Lord." We sang worship songs to the Lord for at least thirty minutes. It was an amazing sight. Hands were lifted all over the room as the audience erupted in praises to God. When I took my seat, several people came by our table to thank me for the music.

One young woman came over and sat down. She asked, "How is it that you, a gospel singer, came to the bar tonight?"

I told her that although Joe had invited me, I really thought God had sent me. I picked up the conversation and said, "If Jesus were in town, this is no doubt where He'd come. Jesus would go wherever people have a desperate need for Him. I guess that's why I'm here tonight: to let people know that if they have a need, Jesus can and will help them."

My guests and I conversed with the young lady, and a few moments later, she bowed her head. Right then and there in the bar, she invited Jesus into her heart.

Another listener stopped by. The young man took a seat at our table and said, "I gave my heart to Jesus when I was a child. Since then, I have walked away from God. But hearing all these great hymns and worship songs tonight has stirred up a longing in my heart."

I explained to the young man that the longing he was feeling was the love of God and the Holy Spirit drawing him back to Jesus. A few moments later, he bowed his head and rededicated his life to Jesus. A few days later, I received a barrage of emails asking me when I was coming back to the bar to jam with the band.

I'll never forget how brightly the light of Christ shined in the bar that night. It's true that light shines brightest against the darkness. But you and I have to flip the switch, turning the light on and, in many cases, turning the light up to maximize every opportunity. We've all heard faith can move mountains. But it's not until hope enters the picture that the mountain of despair begins to move. In unexpected places and unconventional ways, that's what happens when you and I become beacons of light.

The Great Commission

What happened in the bar that night may seem unusual. I don't get invited to sing in bars on a regular basis, though I have been invited to sing in some places that are just as exciting. I've sung in local jails and federal prisons. Street corners, African jungles, and cruise ships. High schools, halfway houses, and hotel ballrooms. It doesn't matter to me. I just want to be willing to go wherever the call of God leads. Shouldn't we all be ready to go where the call of God leads so we can put the name of Jesus in the most favorable light possible? The goal is the worthiest goal ever: to make disciples and help them to grow into mature believers.

There are other passages in the Bible that remind us to let our light "so shine." One of those passages is the Great Commission. After His resurrection, Jesus met with His followers and gave them some parting words:

> And Jesus came and spoke to them, saying, "All authority has been given to Me in heaven and on earth. Go therefore and make disciples of all the nations, baptizing them in the name of the Father and of the Son and of the Holy Spirit, teaching them to observe all things that I have commanded you; and lo, I am with you always, even to the end of the age." Amen.

These verses in Matthew 28:18–20 comprise one of the most important passages in the Bible. And yet a surprising percentage of Christians are unfamiliar with Jesus' famous parting words. According to a 2018 Barna survey, 51 percent of US churchgoers don't recognize the term "the Great Commission." While 17 percent are familiar with the term, they don't know where to find the passage in the Bible. One in four people surveyed (25 percent) said "the Great Commission" rang a bell, but they couldn't remember what it referred to. And 6 percent were not sure whether they had ever heard the term before.[5] These statistics reveal that many Christians are ignorant of the Great Commission and its significance to every believer.

A person's age was also a significant factor in whether churchgoers were familiar with the term. More than one-quarter of the generations known as elders (29 percent) and baby boomers (26 percent) confirmed that they knew the passage, compared to 17 percent of Generation X and 10 percent of millennials.[6] The results of the survey reveal that the term is being used less frequently in our culture, which may mean that teaching on evangelism is becoming less of a priority in the church.

So why is it important to know the Great Commission?

These words of Jesus are a nonnegotiable command to all Christians, recording the final personal directive Jesus gave His disciples. These instructions from the Lord Jesus serve as a clarion call to believers everywhere to carry out the plan that began when God sent His Son, Jesus, into the world. Every believer should consider it a duty and a responsibility to go make disciples, teach the message of the gospel, and encourage new believers to be baptized.

Do you remember who shared the gospel with you? How did you first hear the message of Jesus? Think about it. Someone shared the gospel with the person who led you to Jesus. Then, in turn, that person shared the gospel message with you and led you to Christ. Now you can take part in the process. There is no joy like knowing you are being obedient to the Great Commission of Jesus Christ.

Let's take a closer look at this powerful command from Jesus, understanding that His final assignment to every believer is not optional. The Great Commission is to be taken personally. If we don't share it, then the world won't know.

> And Jesus came and spoke to them, saying, "All authority has been
> given to Me in heaven and on earth. Go therefore and make disciples
> of all the nations, baptizing them in the name of the Father and of
> the Son and of the Holy Spirit, teaching them to observe all things

that I have commanded you; and lo, I am with you always, even to the end of the age." Amen. (Matt. 28:18–20)

Did you notice that the Great Commission is a command and not a suggestion? The word *go* is commonly used in our everyday vocabulary. In fact, according to one online resource, the word *go* is used 1,492 times in the King James Version of the Bible.[7] A small, two-letter word with huge implications, the word *go* means to "change location; move, travel or proceed."[8] Did you notice that all the words in the definition are action verbs? What does God want every believer to do? Not sit down and stay but get up and go! As we change locations from home to work, as we move from place to place, as we travel from the office to the subway, we are to proceed in obedience to God's call, by making disciples for Jesus Christ.

> ## There is no joy like knowing you are being obedient to the Great Commission of Jesus Christ.

May I just put it in plain language? If we are not taking the gospel with us as we change locations, move about in our travels, and proceed with a course of action, then we are disobedient to God's command. Merely thinking about it or planning to do it or getting around to it is delayed obedience. And that is the same as deliberate disobedience. There are no conditions to the Great Commission. Jesus mandated the disciples of old and the church at large today to follow through with His plan. He gave us His official order along with a course of action. God told Abram to go to another country (Gen. 12:1). God told Moses to go deliver His people from bondage (Ex. 3:10). God told Jonah to go preach, as we saw in chapter 2 (Jon. 3:2). God told Paul to get up and go into the city to receive his orders from God (Acts 9:6). Jesus told the blind man to go because his faith had made him well (Mark 10:52). Did you notice that the command to go is always followed by specific instructions? What is God telling you to go and do? Dear one, if you listen closely, God will give you a specific assignment to go and do something great for Him. It's up to us to carry out the Great Commission with great confidence and boldness, knowing we are helping to fulfill this amazing assignment.

Matthew 28:18–20 maps out the purpose of every believer. We are not saved just so we can enjoy the comforts of life. We are saved from sin and the penalty of death. We are saved from hell and eternal separation from God. And we are saved for heaven! We are saved to the glory of God. We are discipled to make disciples. We are loved to love. We are led to lead others to Christ. And we are helped to help those in need.

This little poem helps me simplify and remember the call to shine by sharing the gospel:

> Life is brief.
> And death is sure.
> Sin is the curse.
> Christ is the cure.

After reading the depressing statistics about churchgoers' ignorance of the Great Commission, I am more determined than ever to carry out its call by sharing the gospel with more clarity and urgency.

I present the same challenge to you:

Find Matthew 28:18–20 in your Bible.

Read it.

Highlight it.

Learn it.

Memorize it.

Fulfill it.

Shine with Intensity

Light is meant to be seen by people who live in darkness. A light that is covered up or hidden has no value and does not serve the purpose for which it was created. The Bible encourages us to shine our light by putting our good works on display—not so we can take the credit, but so God can receive glory.

We know that every word in the Bible is significant. If you read a little farther in Matthew 5, you'll find these words: "Not even a period or comma will ever disappear from the Law. Everything written in it must happen" (v. 18 CEV). In the Bible, every phrase, each word, and even the punctuation marks have significance. The dot of an *i* and the cross of a *t* in the Scriptures carry weight and meaning.

Nestled in Matthew 5:16 is another two-letter word with a great big meaning. It's the word *so*. It means "to such a great extent. Extremely, very much"[9] and "to a very great degree."[10] Think of it as "beyond any doubt." This two-letter word gives us a huge indication of the intensity, the strength, or the magnitude of our personal, individual lights. It's all about helping people find hope. I discovered a great acronym for hope: Hold On Pain Ends. That's what we are supposed to do—let people know that there is something extremely good just around the next corner.

The intensity of your light is proportionate to the intensity of your love. You cannot have love for others without the love of Christ. Some days, shining your light may mean going out of your way to meet someone's need or have an important conversation about Jesus with a friend or loved one. On another occasion, it may mean putting extra effort into a ministry assignment or mission project. On yet another occasion, turning up the intensity of your light may mean putting more money in the offering plate to support the work of a specific ministry.

Whatever work you are doing, don't do it halfheartedly. Work at it with a passion. Put your heart and soul into it. If the intensity of your light is proportionate to the intensity of your love, then those who are on the receiving end of your efforts are certain to receive a huge blessing all because of you. You'll find one of the best ways to bless God is to be a blessing to one of His children.

The intensity of your light is proportionate to the intensity of your love.

There's another Bible verse that highlights the simple but profound use of the word *so*. We looked at it briefly in chapter 1. John 3:16 says, "For God *so* loved the world that He gave His only begotten Son, that whoever believes in Him should not perish but have everlasting life." A strong connection can be made between Matthew 5:16 and John 3:16. Jesus loved us to such an extent that He laid down His life for us when He was crucified on the cross for our sins. That display of love changed our destiny forever. In response to this great love God has for us, we should be overwhelmed with gratitude and ready to let our lights shine to the greatest degree everywhere we go.

I hope you see the connection between God's love and the privilege of shining for Him. It's His great love for you that influences how you shine your light for Christ. If you desire to shine your light with more intensity, begin by praying for boldness to be ready at any moment to speak up for Christ. Trust that God will give you opportunities to share your faith in Christ.

Shine with Great Integrity

What is *biblical* integrity? And how will it help you shine brighter?

First, let's talk about the root of the word. The word *integrity* originates from *integer*, meaning "whole" or "complete."[11] *Integrity* means possessing qualities of "honesty," "sound moral principle," and "uprightness."[12] Certified public accountant and international speaker Deborah Pegues underscores the fact that a person who lacks integrity can't expect God to bless their efforts. She says, "You can't expect to prosper if you are doing dishonest things.... Integrity is integrating what I say I believe with what I do."[13] So, putting integrity into perspective, integrity means focusing on doing the right thing for the right reason. One of my favorite preachers and authors, Dr. Myles Munroe, said this: "A person with character does not live on what's popular; they live on what is principle."[14]

Years ago, when I first started teaching school, I had a music student in my class we'll call Arnie. He grew to be a very talented musician with a promising career ahead of him. One day Arnie made a very bad decision that landed him in prison where he is now serving a lengthy sentence. I have received letters from Arnie with updates on how he is doing. Over the years, he has grown in his faith. He leads the music for the prison's Sunday morning worship services, and he often leads a Bible study for his fellow inmates. As his former teacher and friend, I have written Arnie on occasion to remind him to stay true to his faith in Christ, to caution him to remain honest and forthright in his dealings, and to encourage him to use his gifts for God, even under adverse circumstances.

Not long ago I got a letter from Arnie containing an interesting story. One day while he and some of his fellow inmates were gathered in the prison's common area where there was a television on the wall, a popular gospel music program came on the air. It happened to be an episode where I was featured as one of the guest singers.

Arnie shouted to his friends, "Hey, that's my friend Babbie Mason up there singing on the television."

His friends didn't believe that he knew me, and they shouted him down. Arnie was disappointed that he was not able to convince his buddies he knew me—until the next day when he received one of my personal letters of encouragement. Arnie showed his friends my letter. He said that it wasn't so much that he needed to convince his fellow inmates that he knew me but that he welcomed the encouragement I shared with him to remain a godly, upright man—the kind of man God is looking for. Arnie sensed the presence of God and a renewed hope that he was not alone in that great big prison.

Now listen, dear friend. I know I am just flesh and blood like everyone else. But it is such an honor to hear that someone's load got a little lighter upon hearing the name of a good friend. Will you join me in asking God for a name and a reputation that brings honor to *His* name? Proverbs 22:1 says, "Choose a good reputation over great riches; being held in high esteem is better than silver or gold" (NLT).

It's possible that even right now, someone is mentioning your name in a conversation. Maybe they are remarking about a kind word you spoke or a good deed you performed. Maybe they mentioned you in their prayers. How does it make you feel, knowing that someone may have called your name when they gave God thanks? Pretty humbling, isn't it? You may have just been following the Lord's leading. But actually, you were aligning your actions with your words. That is what integrity is. It means uprightness of character or action. It means trustworthy and responsible.

Wisdom is knowing the right direction to take. Integrity follows the path one step at a time. Psalm 16:8 is of great encouragement: "I keep my eyes always on the LORD. With Him at my right hand, I will not be shaken" (NIV).

When we walk in integrity, we live our lives as a whole. We know what's right; then we do what's right. We operate with integrity when our actions align with our words. Proclaiming the truth and not doing it is called *hypocrisy*. It's putting on a mask and faking it, appearing to be someone you are not. That is a lack of integrity. When we compartmentalize our lives, we reveal our weaknesses and vulnerabilities. A person who lacks integrity will eventually crack under pressure; her true character will emerge, revealing who she really is. That person will make poor decisions that disappoint others. She will become a disappointment to herself. Ultimately, this lack of integrity will impact her testimony, her reputation, and her relationship with God.

I found that the word *holy*, similar to *integrity*, means that which is "properly, whole, entire or perfect."[15] We can't say we love a holy and righteous God—the God who is spirit and truth—and live a life of dishonesty. Those two actions are counterintuitive. They are not compatible. We are one people, set apart as shown in Deuteronomy 6:4: "Hear, O Israel: The LORD our God is one LORD" (KJV). A person with integrity is a person with single-minded character.

How does all this integrate with shining your light? Shining your light is the best way you can put your testimony in the spotlight. We all know that people can see right through someone who is putting on airs. It's not a secret. When our actions don't line up with our words, everyone knows it! We must always remember who we represent. Jesus, the personification of integrity, is the same yesterday, today, and forever (see Mal. 3:6; Heb. 13:8). When you represent Christ, you are representing truth and integrity. That means doing the right thing for the right reasons. Proverbs 11:3 echoes this sentiment: "The integrity of the upright guides them, but the unfaithful are destroyed by their duplicity" (NIV).

Shine with Great Intention

The commitment displayed to the Waodani by the Elliots and others impacted an entire nation for Christ. Their dedication to missions stands unparalleled in modern times. They were obedient to a specific calling from God, even to the point of putting their lives on the line. They exemplified what it means to be fully present. Jim Elliot said it best: "Wherever you are, *be all there*. Live to the hilt every situation you believe to be the will of God."[16]

What about you? What is God calling you to do?

Your response is to pray and ask God to clearly reveal His mission for *you*. Imagine the impact we could have in our neighborhoods, our schools, and our churches if we actually prayed and asked God to reveal His purpose for us. Then, after praying, imagine what it would look like if we actually followed through in obedience!

Matthew 5:15 has something to say about intention: "And people don't hide a light under a bowl. They put it on a lampstand so the light shines for all the people in the house" (NCV). A woman who places her lamp under a bowl may wish to conceal it. Why would she do that? Maybe she is afraid of negative repercussions. Maybe she puts her lamp under a bowl because she is too busy at the moment, so she covers her light with the intention of coming back to it later. Or perhaps she puts her light under a bowl out of embarrassment. She doesn't want others to see her light. Too concerned with what others may think, she compares her light to those around her and puts her light away in shame.

If you are fearful or hesitant to share your faith with others, be honest with yourself. You know where you fall short. Then be honest with God. He already knows of your lack of confidence in this area. Ask Him to help you, and He will. You'll find great courage in these verses: "Ask, and it will be given to you; seek, and you will find; knock, and it will be opened to you. For everyone who asks receives, and he who seeks finds, and to him who knocks it will be opened" (Matthew 7:7–8). If you desire to do your part in fulfilling the Great Commission, Jesus, through the power of the Holy

Spirit, will help you to be obedient to this call. You have a unique and wonderful role to play. You only need to ask God where to begin.

Shine Despite Interruptions

The opportunities to share may not always come in a nice, neat package. At a glance, an opportunity may appear more like an obstacle. As you keep your heart open to God's direction, ask God to lead you to people and situations where you can make a difference. When those opportunities arise, pray for wisdom, boldness, and discernment as you interact with others. Remember, shining your light for Christ is a lifelong journey that is filled with joy and expectation. Stay committed, be authentic, and trust that God will use your efforts to impact the people around you.

What do you imagine your day would look like if every part of it—including each interruption—was totally yielded to God? I don't know about you, but I plan my daily activities by the appointments, meetings, and obligations I've scheduled on my calendar. However, almost daily, there are interruptions and changes to my plans. I'll be honest with you; I sometimes see interruptions as annoyances or intrusions on my plans. Some days, I have to throw my plans completely out the window, so to speak, because of unexpected diversions. Has any of this ever happened to you? We can take comfort though. Jesus was often interrupted during the course of His day. Jesus shows us that what we call an interruption can actually be a divine appointment.

Jesus had become such a popular figure that throngs of people followed Him wherever He went. Imagine the crowds of people appealing to Jesus for food, words of wisdom, healing, and solutions to their problems. In Mark 2:1–12, we read of the account where, one day, Jesus was teaching a huge crowd of people inside of a house. Jesus' lesson was interrupted when the ceiling of the house fell in. Right in the middle of His teaching, four men lowered their paralyzed friend through a hole in the roof. Jesus didn't respond with anger because of the interruption. Nor was

He short-tempered because of the delay. But, with compassion, Jesus welcomed the opportunity to demonstrate forgiveness and healing to the lame man, who took up his mat and went to his own house rejoicing.

On another occasion, in Mark 4:35–41, we read that Jesus was in a boat with His disciples on a huge lake. Suddenly, a storm rose up. The raging waters and the dashing waves began to toss the boat so violently that the disciples were struck with terror. They thought they were going to die. Jesus, exhausted from His work, was trying to get some much-needed rest in the hull of the boat. But His sleep was interrupted by the disciples, who were in a state of panic. Jesus spoke peace not only to the troubled hearts of the disciples but also to the raging waters beneath them.

Some days, Jesus was interrupted in the middle of being interrupted. In Mark 5, after Jesus had calmed the storm, He was getting out of the boat onto the shore when He was interrupted by a huge crowd. A rich man by the name of Jairus got through the crowd to have an audience with Jesus because of his important position in the community. Jairus asked Jesus to come to His house to heal his daughter. Jesus agreed to visit the man's sick daughter. He was on His way to where she was, but with the press of the crowd, He noticed that someone had touched Him—someone with tremendous need and, more than that, with tremendous faith. Jesus asked who touched Him, and we learn that it was a woman who had been sick with a bleeding disorder for twelve years. This woman who had been outcast and ostracized knew that Jesus could heal her. And He did. This collision of interruptions demonstrates that Jesus will always take time to care for the broken, the sick, and the downtrodden, regardless of who they are or their station in life.

There is a great lesson we can learn from interruptions. We see interruptions as inconveniences. But God sees them as interventions—a way He can orchestrate His will and purpose in our lives. He desires that we give Him complete freedom to design our everyday lives so that at any moment we can be used by Him to shine our lights on others.

Shining God's Light to the World

God's plan for our lives could take us anywhere at a moment's notice. Acts 1:8 tells us that the Great Commission could take us across town, across the state, across the region, across the country, across the continent, or across the world: "But ye shall receive power, after that the Holy Ghost is come upon you: and ye shall be witnesses unto me both in Jerusalem, and in all Judaea, and in Samaria, and unto the uttermost part of the earth" (KJV). In some instances, you may go personally to accomplish the mission. If you are not able to go, you can send someone by supporting their missionary efforts. Like Jairus, could you stretch your faith just a little more? Like the woman with the issue of blood, can you believe God for greater miracles? Like the guys who lowered their friend through the roof, can you be just a little bolder in your faith walk? Walking by faith is where you will begin to see how big your God really is.

Sometimes we drag our feet and let good intentions fade. We need to put ourselves in places where we can be encouraged to continue shining our lights. I have always been blessed by the preaching ministry of Dr. Charles Stanley. He was the founder of In Touch Ministries and the pastor of First Baptist Atlanta until his death in 2023. It has been my joy to sing at First Baptist Atlanta on many occasions. In his book *God's Way Day by Day*, Dr. Stanley says, "What God calls us to do may not make sense. We may be able to come up with all sorts of excuses for not obeying. In the end, however, there's only one wise choice. Obey God."[17]

Intention and obedience are like twin sisters whose combined efforts can really get things done. When you live with intention and obedience, you live with a distinct purpose as you walk by faith. Everything you do matters. So raise your light high and shine with a passion. How or when or for whom you shine is not your concern. Whether you are sure of the way or not, your only intention and call is to obey God and leave the outcome to Him.

Reflections

Here is an assignment for today. Shining your light to the greatest extent takes total dependence on God to lead and guide you. Pause and think about the price Jesus paid for your salvation. Consider all the benefits you have because of what Jesus has done for you.

> You are forgiven of sin.
> You have a home in heaven for all eternity.
> You have an overabundance of love from God.
> You have all the fruit of the Spirit.
> You have a renewed sense of purpose and calling.
> You have a reason to live and the greatest message in the
>   world to share!

All of that, my friend, is something to be so very excited about. Today, let's close our session with a prayer for boldness to answer God's call wherever He leads.

> Most gracious Father, thank You for being strong and mighty in my life. No one and no thing can come against You; therefore, nothing can come against me because greater are You on the inside of me than he that is in the world. And because You are awesome on the inside of me, no power can come against me and prevail. Neither will my heart be weakened by fear of men. I confess that I walk in the boldness and the fearlessness of a lion today. With great courage and confidence, help me to proclaim Your

love and salvation to the furthest extent and beyond any doubt. Give me the words to say and the compassion to act. I will not cower in the face of adversity but seize every moment to make Your name great here on the earth. And I will do it with great joy and thanksgiving. In Christ's name, amen.

Chapter 5

Give Your Light Away

*Let your light so shine **before men**,*
that they may see your good works and
glorify your Father in heaven.

Matthew 5:16

Recalling the numerous occasions where I have shared my faith as I come and go, I see a reoccurring pattern. I seem to easily connect with people in places like the grocery store, the pharmacy, the gas station, and the department store. I think I have found the key to my style of evangelism: to let my light so shine—I should go shopping!

It's kind of funny when you look at it that way. But there is an important point that applies to you as much as it applies to me. To fulfill the Great Commission, we have to go where the people are. Have you noticed that Jesus was drawn to people and people were drawn to Him? John Wesley, an evangelist who lived during the eighteenth century, is credited with this insight: "Untold millions are still untold." People still need the Lord, and the gospel is still a message for this mess age. Wherever it is that you connect with people, take the message of Jesus with you. Shining your light means meeting the needs of people with the love of God. That's where you and I will experience the wonderful adventures of sharing Jesus.

Speaking of adventure, an unforgettable connection comes flooding into my mind right now. As you read it, keep in mind that Jesus is all about people. Once people encounter Jesus, they are never the same. Wouldn't you agree? Everything is better with Jesus. Let me tell you about a conversation that had eternal value.

About fourteen years ago, I made a quick stop at the grocery store. While I was filling my cart, I heard the voice of a small child one aisle over. She was singing along with the music playing on the store's sound system. The little one wasn't just singing. She was *singing*! With total abandon, this precious girl was singing every word, and her sweet voice was music to my ears. I couldn't help but go find her; the sound of kids singing just calls to this old schoolteacher's heart. (I often tell people I taught "mental high school music" because you have to be part crazy to teach eleven-, twelve-, and thirteen-year-olds on a daily basis! Seriously, I loved every minute of it. Many of my middle school students remain close friends to this day.)

I was so smitten by the little girl's singing voice, I stopped in my tracks. Her pitch was dead-on, and her diction was impeccable for a young child. I wheeled my cart around the corner to the next aisle so I could meet this precious little star singer personally. When I caught her eye, she realized that her singing was attracting attention, and she sheepishly brought her performance to a screeching halt.

She appeared to be in early grade school, maybe six or seven years old. She was pushing the grocery cart while a gentleman I assumed was her father took items from the shelf and placed them in their cart.

I just had to speak up. "Excuse me, sir, but I couldn't help but overhear your daughter's singing voice from the next aisle. You have quite a little singer there." The gentleman beamed with pride. If you want to really be a blessing to a parent, say something positive about their children.

He took the compliment and ran with it. "Yeah, my little girl was singing at the top of her lungs even before she could talk. She loves music."

"I know what you mean," I replied. "I'm a singer and a music teacher, and I know a potential star when I hear one." I pleaded with him as our conversation continued: "Please keep her involved in music. Okay? You might want to consider getting her a good piano teacher or make sure she gets in the school choir and church's youth choir. If she's still singing like that in a few years, I recommend that you get her a good voice coach. Just keep this child in music because it's quite obvious she loves it, and she's definitely got the gift."

The little girl was a bit shy at first, but she opened up the more we conversed. She seemed to relish the fact that I enjoyed her singing. Her bright eyes lit up when I recommended music lessons and singing in the church kid's choir.

Fast-forward fourteen years. I was at the doctor's office recently, and I stopped by the counter to make my next appointment. A young lady spoke up from behind the desk. "Hello, Mrs. Mason, I have a quick question for you. Do you remember years ago when you were out shopping and you heard a little girl singing at the top of her lungs in the next aisle?"

I took the story up from there and continued, "Yes, and if I remember correctly, I spoke to her dad and told him how much I enjoyed his daughter's singing voice and to get that little girl in some music lessons and the church youth choir. Right?"

She raised her eyebrows along with the pitch in her voice. "Exactly, exactly! Well, that little girl was me! I was only a kid back then, but you told my daddy to keep me involved in music. I want you to know that I'm working here at the doctor's office during the week, but I sing every Sunday when I lead worship in my church. Thanks for encouraging me, even way back then."

Needless to say, I was blown away. First of all, I was surprised that I remembered that incident as if it were yesterday. And I couldn't believe that the Lord would connect us after so many years. Even more, I was astonished that the young lady was all grown up and serving the Lord on the worship team in a neighborhood church! God is truly amazing, isn't He?

That unexpected meeting was not by chance. The Lord reminded me that every one of us has a role to play in winning people to Him. Because the Lord allowed us to meet that day many years ago, I was able to plant a seed of encouragement in a daughter's heart—as well as her daddy's. Along the way, someone led them to the Lord, and now they are growing in their faith and involved in their church. I don't know who, but obviously someone acknowledged her ability to sing and gave the young lady a place to serve on the church worship team.

We touched on this in the introduction, but I want to park here for a moment. I'll say it again: *Everything you do for Christ matters.*

You might plant the seed by speaking a kind word, or, as in my case, you may take a moment to encourage a family or share a simple compliment. You may water the seed when you sit down face to face and actually pray the prayer of salvation with someone, leading them to the Lord. (See the "Prayer of Salvation and Memory Verses" chapter.) But it's God who causes these seeds to grow and bear fruit.

Everything you do for Christ matters.

Read this key verse written by the apostle Paul, and as you do, consider its application. It's found in 1 Corinthians 3:6–7: "I planted the seed in your hearts, and Apollos watered it, but it was God who made it grow. It's not important who does the planting, or who does the watering. What's important is that God makes the seed grow" (NLT).

It's imperative that we know what the apostle Paul was saying here. Throughout his letter to the Corinthian church, Paul spoke to disunity and division in the church. He said the believers there behaved like little children who acted foolishly because they focused more on whose teaching they followed, Paul's or Apollos's, rather than on more important matters, such as working together to promote the message of the gospel.

As Paul continued his teaching, he set the record straight: "The one who plants and the one who waters work together with the same purpose" (v. 8 NLT). Paul emphasized that he and Apollos were merely servants that God was using to bring the people of Corinth to faith in Christ Jesus. The leaders' individual teaching styles weren't the focus. Their backgrounds and credentials were impressive but not important. The gospel message should always be the focus. It doesn't matter if you plant the seed or water it, as long as God gets the glory.

To break it down into modern-day vernacular, "get in where you fit in." We're all on the same team. It's Jesus' name that we celebrate.

Doing What Jesus Did

So, in your case, what would it look like to take Jesus to the world where you live? Whose life would be encouraged if you shared God's love in the marketplace? How could you impact your coworkers with more kindness in the workplace? Thinking ahead, imagine how you could be a blessing by offering to pray for your server the next time you eat out. How would your neighborhood be changed for the better by inviting your neighbor to church? In this chapter, we'll consider the next phrase in the Great Mandate from Matthew 5:16, "Let your light so shine *before men*." Consider what it would look like to shine your light before the people you encounter on a day-by-day basis. Simply put, we have no influence without involvement. You can't rescue people from a burning building without getting close enough to feel the intense heat from the blaze. And you cannot save a drowning man without getting drenched by ocean waves. To bring hope to others, we have to get involved.

That's what Charles did for more than twenty years. He got involved in the lives of kids as a Little League baseball coach. As a matter of fact, the East Marietta National Little League team from Marietta, Georgia, won the League World Series in 1983, bringing the pennant to the United States, beating out the Little League team from the Dominican Republic.

Several of Charles's players were on the team that year. Many of the kids he coached on the ball field were the same kids I taught in the classroom. They're all grown up now. Today, we attend church together. Charles and I have attended their weddings. We support their ministries. We've met and encouraged their kids. Why? Because when we do life together, it creates and strengthens a lifelong connection that brings joy and significance to life. It was a privilege for Charles and me to teach kids about the fundamentals of music and baseball. I believe they also learned something about how to navigate life.

That's what Jesus does. In the New Testament, wherever there are people, you'll find Jesus doing life with them. You will find Jesus walking in His calling to love His neighbors, rescue the perishing, and care for the dying. Let's look at how Jesus got involved with people who had big life-and-death issues.

Luke 7 records the story of a widow who was on her way to bury her son. When Jesus met this broken woman, He discovered that she stood to lose much more than just the son she treasured so much. Her financial future, her home, her name, and her inheritance were all at stake.

Let's read her story:

Soon afterward Jesus went with his disciples to the village of Nain, and a large crowd followed him. A funeral procession was coming out as he approached the village gate. The young man who had died was a widow's only son, and a large crowd from the village was with her. When the Lord saw her, his heart overflowed with compassion. "Don't cry!" he said. Then he walked over to the coffin and touched it, and the bearers stopped. "Young man," he said, "I tell you, get up." Then the dead boy sat up and began to talk! And Jesus gave him back to his mother.

Great fear swept the crowd, and they praised God, saying, "A mighty prophet has risen among us," and "God has visited his people today." And the news about Jesus spread throughout Judea and the surrounding countryside. (vv. 11–17 NLT)

This nameless woman no doubt had nothing to look forward to except pain and regret. But Jesus came to the widow's aid at just the time she needed Him most. He got involved.

Jesus Engages with People in Crisis

As Jesus was approaching the city of Nain, He met a funeral procession. Most of us have experienced the loss of a loved one, and it's a sad affair. Here in the South, when a funeral procession is approaching on the street, all the drivers on the road pull over to the side to allow the procession to pass by uninterrupted out of respect for the dead. In that moment, everyone can feel the weight of pain and discouragement for the families and friends who have lost a loved one.

The pain of the widow of Nain was fresh. In this case, the deceased young man was her only child. And we know he had died that day because according to Deuteronomy

21:23 and Acts 5:5–10, a corpse had to be buried the same day. This woman was now all alone. She had no other family. The implication here is tremendous. There were no social agencies to take care of widows in those days. She had no more options.[1]

With no more hope, she could look forward only to financial ruin, starvation, and death. (Remember the stories of Naomi in the book of Ruth and the woman from Zarephath in 1 Kings 17:8–16? Those widows found themselves in similar circumstances.)

At just the right moment, when the pallbearers were carrying the young man's body to the graveyard, Jesus met the widowed mother. The Bible says that Jesus had compassion on her and told her not to cry (Luke 7:13).

This is what I love about Jesus. He is not an observer. He doesn't stand idly by, spectating. He doesn't wait for somebody to make the first move. Instead, He immediately got involved and stepped in to comfort the widowed mother. Today, we hear a lot about the word *engaged*. The word means "fully occupied" or having one's "full attention."[2] This is a word of comfort to us. When we are in pain, Jesus takes notice and becomes fully involved. We are always on His radar. Jesus saw the woman following behind her dead son's coffin. He saw that the woman's face was streaked with tears. He sensed her grief-stricken heart and her broken spirit. He sympathized with her desperation and her imminent crisis.

What did Jesus do? *He met her need by comforting her.*

Jesus Empathizes with People Who Are Broken

Imagine Jesus as He took this widowed woman by the hands to express His condolences for her loss. Having buried both of my parents, and having experienced the pain of that deep grief, just imagining this show of empathy is enough to bring me to tears. I know personally that the pain of grief is real.

Anyone who has ever lost a loved one can understand that you never really recover from certain losses. You can get through it, but you never get over it. Can you relate?

Our precious Lord, Jesus, can. He understands this kind of grief and loss. Isaiah 53:3 tells us that Jesus "was despised and rejected—a man of sorrows, acquainted with deepest grief" (NLT). The Bible tells us that Jesus not only bore our sins but also carried our sorrows to the cross. Jesus carried the weight of the whole world on His shoulders.

Take comfort, dear one. If life has caused you pain and grief, Jesus knows all about it. And He cares. Hebrews 4:15 tells us that Jesus feels our pain and frailties: "For we do not have a high priest who is unable to empathize with our weaknesses, but we have one who has been tempted in every way, just as we are—yet he did not sin" (NIV).

Let's put it in today's vocabulary: "Jesus has been there." And because He has been there, He touches broken lives and ruined dreams at the point of our deepest pain. He wasn't concerned with ceremonial uncleanness but walked up and touched a dead man's coffin.

In his book *Where Is God When It Hurts?*, author Philip Yancey helps readers cope with physical and emotional pain. He says, "The first step in healing a suffering person ... is to acknowledge that the pain is valid, and worthy of a sympathetic response."[3] In fact, that is what Luke 7:13 implies. Jesus doesn't hurry us through the process of dealing with pain. He doesn't treat you coldly or distantly, as if to say, "Keep a stiff upper lip. Deal with it." No. Through His ever-present promises, Jesus meets you right in the middle of the mess. He wraps His arms around you and says, "Do not cry."

If life has caused you pain and grief, Jesus knows all about it. And He cares.

Jesus Elevates People Who Are Downcast

We must see the account of the widow as more than just a Sunday school lesson. This story is real. And it's probably real to you in one sense or another. When you read about the miracles of Jesus, you will see people at a point of desperation. He gave sight to the blind. He touched and healed the leper. He raised Lazarus from the dead. He healed the woman who had been sick for twelve years with a blood disorder. He delivered a man possessed by evil spirits. He calmed a furious storm on the Sea of Galilee. And to meet a sinful world's greatest need, Jesus conquered death.

To Jesus, no one is less than. He treats us all equally, and He treats us all with dignity. As a woman, I know what it's like to be devalued and overlooked. As a Black woman, I know the sting of racism and prejudice. As a woman in ministry, I have felt disdain and condescension from men who considered me inferior and patronized me. Maybe you have been there too. If you have, Jesus lifts us up from our low position and raises us up above our circumstances to a place of victory.

You may have heard the old saying that God helps those who help themselves. That may be true in some situations, but there are many more examples of God helping those who are completely helpless. He loves to help the weak, and He gives strength to those who have none. Jesus encourages us when we are worn to a frazzle, disappointed by loved ones, and betrayed by those we thought we could trust. Here's the long and short of it: God is a God of miracles. He parts the seas, He feeds multitudes, and He lifts up those who are too weak to help themselves.

When I think of broken people, I can't help but think of the nursery rhyme "Humpty Dumpty" and the line,

All the King's horses and all the King's men
Cannot put Humpty Dumpty together again.[4]

But King Jesus can! And He uses people to do it. That means we have to be available to serve others. Jesus is not a long-distance God. He is a friend who "sticks closer than a brother" (Prov. 18:24). Therefore, we need to do everything we can to come alongside people in a warm, personal, and friendly way, pushing back against a culture of distancing and online isolation.

We can also be the first to notice the good things people do and encourage them to continue doing good. First Thessalonians reminds us to speak words that uplift others: "So speak encouraging words to one another. Build up hope so you'll all be together in this, no one left out, no one left behind. I know you're already doing this; just keep on doing it" (5:11 MSG).

Shine your light in a broken world. It will make a difference.

Build Face-to-Face Connections

When Jesus walked the earth, He prioritized face-to-face connection. Nothing can take its place, especially if a person is hurting. It's not a coincidence that Generation Z, which is the most connected generation through social media, is also considered the loneliest. So how do we turn this around? We can make every effort to create time for face-to-face conversations.

It only takes a few moments to engage. When you see someone who is hurting, don't give them the side eye. Slow up. Acknowledge their presence. Pay attention to their response. Take time to engage with friends and even strangers by giving them your full and undivided attention. When you are in a conversation, limit any distractions, such as the temptation to check your phone or look off in another direction. Do your best to avoid anything that may keep you from total engagement. You never know how your conversation could provide the uplift and encouragement someone might need to get through a difficult moment. This is the time to provide a friend with your complete attention, affirming that you're not only listening to them but also hearing what they have to say.

Look for Places to Serve

Let me tell you a little more about Charles. He is kind, generous, and my biggest supporter. Our marriage is "interesting," though, because we are total opposites in many respects. I'm from the North. He is southern born and bred. I'm a city girl. Charles is country to the core. I like the indoors, where you'll find me writing a song from the piano, working on a chapter for a book, or redecorating a room. Charles likes the outdoors, where you'll find him tending to his garden, catching fish, or feeding his chickens. I like chocolate. Charles's favorite flavor is vanilla. Charles wants a kosher dill pickle with his burger. I've gotta have sweet bread-and-butter pickles. I prefer to rise early. Charles likes sleeping in. I like trivia game shows. He likes cowboy Westerns. I like long walks. He likes catnaps.

It's comedic that we are so opposite. But when it comes to our love for Christ, we are definitely on the same page. We love our church and finding places to serve there. He travels with me when we tour for ministry, and I've taken notes on how easily he shares his love for Christ at home or when we are on the road.

When Charles and I go out to eat, he always asks the servers if they go to church. He'll say something like this: "My wife is a gospel singer." (It's kind of embarrassing sometimes because I'm his favorite singer. It makes me blush, but I can handle it for the sake of the gospel.) "You should come to our church soon to hear her lead the singing." That always seems to welcome interesting conversation. Then we'll leave a card with my website information along with a generous tip. (By the way, I often hear that Christians are the worst tippers. That's not a good representation, so let's do our best to work on changing it. Being generous is always a good thing.) Again, it's a simple point that is easy to execute. First Corinthians 10:24 says, "Let no one seek his own good, but the good of his neighbor" (ESV). Shining your light means reaching people with love and compassion.

Elevate Others

How does this apply? Think about the gifts, talents, or resources you have to contribute. Those gifts are entrusted to you by God to be shared with others. We all have a part of ourselves we can give away to others. As a career coach, I mentor a lot of Christian singers, songwriters, authors, and speakers in my work. Here's a suggestion for musicians and performers who, like me, are looking for audiences to share their talents with. Some of the most memorable concerts I've experienced have been in places where the audience couldn't come to me. So I went to them.

Those audiences may be at a local women's shelter, halfway house, pregnancy resource center, senior adult facility, or local church Sunday school class. I have visited all of these places, as well as men's and women's jails and prisons. There were times I was invited. Then there were times I garnered a bit of boldness, picked up the phone, and called the director of the organization or ministry to ask if I could pay their residents a visit. Most times my phone call was welcomed, and we were able to schedule a visit. In the hour or so we spent worshipping together, not only was the music and worship a blessing to them, but I also came away blessed.

Putting it simply: Make the effort to lift people up. When you lift others, your own troubles become lighter. It doesn't take a lot of effort to be a big blessing. Think of individuals in your neighborhood or apartment complex who may be forgotten or in some way may have fallen between the cracks. No doubt there is an elderly neighbor or a single mother you could invite to church soon. You won't know the outcome until you make the effort. Think about it this way—the next time you are tempted to ignore a stranger or look the other way when approached by someone considered "less than," ask yourself: If that person were Billy Graham, Michael Jordan, or the president of the United States, would you take time to engage them? Regardless of who they are or their circumstances, everyone deserves to be treated with honor and respect.

Colossians 3:23 describes just such an effort: "Work willingly at whatever you do, as though you were working for the Lord rather than for people" (NLT). What part of you can you give away today? Can you be on the lookout (BOLO) for people who are downcast and do your best to lift them up?

Engage. Empathize. Elevate. How can you put those action words into practice? You never know how your efforts, along with the Holy Spirit's help, can make someone's day—maybe even be a lifeline. Let me close this chapter by sharing a story of how the Lord allowed an encouraging word and an engaging song to elevate a woman out of the pit of her despair. This story took place a few years ago, before email and internet streaming were common. But the bottom line of the story is that the Holy Spirit is able to bring people to Jesus; He can work in any kind of situation to rescue people from the brink of despair.

I had been invited to be the guest singer for an event called Friday Night Sing, hosted by Moody Radio in Chicago. The live concert was held in the beautiful sanctuary of the Moody Church and was broadcast simultaneously over more than seventy Moody Radio stations and more than one thousand affiliates. During my concert, I sang a song called "He'll Find a Way," written by my dearest longtime friend and songwriting buddy, Donna Douglas Walchle. The song's encouraging message speaks to how God can find a way where there seems to be no way. The lyrics to the chorus say this:

For I know that if He can paint a sunset
And put the stars in place
I know if He can raise up mountains
And calm the storm-tossed waves

If He can conquer death forever
To open heaven's gates
Then I know for you, I know for you
He'll find a way[5]

A young woman who had heard the concert over the radio in Chicago wrote me a letter the following week. She explained on that Friday night she had been deeply discouraged. She was tired of fighting the multitude of never-ending challenges she had been facing, and she'd decided to end her life. She packed a loaded gun in her purse, got in her car, and headed for Lake Michigan. She reached the shore and sat in her car, contemplating her next move.

To distract herself from all the mixed-up thoughts running rampant through her mind, she turned on the radio in her car. Not really sure of what kind of music to listen to, she hit the scan button. Her car radio landed on my live concert from the Moody Church. The song grabbed her attention, and she listened to the words and music.

In her letter she described how, in that moment, her heart filled with hope. She knew it was a divine moment. She got out of her car with the gun in hand. She walked to the shoreline of the lake and, with all her might, threw it into the deep waters of Lake Michigan. In that moment, she cried out to God to save her. He was right there with her when she needed Him most. Not only did God save her life in that moment, but He also saved her for all eternity.

That amazing story took place only because of the Holy Spirit's powerful interces-sion; He orchestrated the details that saved that young lady's life. You see, I don't always know what to say or sing during my concerts. And I can't begin to know all the needs that are represented among the people who listen to my music or read my books. But I always depend on the Holy Spirit's power to help me, in my weakness, carry out the ministry He has assigned to me. I open my mouth to sing and speak, but it is God, through the power of the Holy Spirit, who allows the words to penetrate the hearts of people who are on the receiving end.

One of the ways God allows me to spread the gospel is though my music. Donna Douglas Walchle and I have written many songs across the years. The song "Love Like That" is a more recent composition that encourages us to love the way Jesus would love. I want to close this chapter with the words to "Love Like That." Sometimes the best prayer is a song. Will you join me in making this song our deepest desire and the prayer of our hearts? Let the words serve as a reminder that to make an impact on the lives of people, you don't have to be perfect or have a big bank account. You don't need to be a Hollywood celebrity or have a face that everyone recognizes. You just have to care.

What would it mean to that single mom
To get some money in the mail
Or pay a visit to Mr. Jones
Whose health has begun to fail
Just to shine a little light
Tell 'em it will be all right

And what about that lonely child
Who's never had enough
Got a kind and encouraging word
For that girl who's given up
Oh what a difference it would make
Just to bless somebody's day

Chorus
Teach me to love like that
Tell me what to say to help my neighbor
Teach me to love like that
Show me what to do to make things better
Maybe it's to fill a need
Or plant a seed
Or give where there is lack
I want to be like You, Lord
Teach me to love like that[6]

Reflections

1. How easy is it for you to engage with others? In what way can you make connecting with others a more deliberate exercise?

2. What new habit can you practice to help you engage with others?

3. What is one small step you can take to cultivate empathy?

4. What is a lesson you have learned when you *didn't* ease someone's pain, empathize with their grief, or elevate them up and out of their pit of discouragement?

5. How may being too busy to engage with others take away from your enjoyment of life?

6. What is one of your positive personal qualities you can use to uplift others?

Chapter 6

Can I Get a Witness?

Let your light so shine before men,
that they may see *your good works and*
glorify your Father in heaven.

Matthew 5:16

The church I grew up in through my young adult years was a neighborhood fellowship made up of everyday, hardworking, blue-collar Black families. Most adults in the church had come to Michigan from the Deep South. They had grown up in the cotton fields of states such as Mississippi, Alabama, Arkansas, and Tennessee—states that were (and in many ways still are) hostile to Black people. Their shotgun houses had no indoor plumbing. They often had to "rob Peter to pay Paul," but God always provided for them. When they told their testimonies, they spoke of how God had tended to them and cared for them during the hardest of times.

As a young, impressionable believer, I marveled at their ability to duck, dodge, and bounce back from whatever life threw at them. The deacons, the choir, the church mothers, the ushers, the faithful church members—they are my Mount Rushmore. Their life stories are forever etched in my memory. I can imagine their busts chiseled into the side of a mountain. They are monumental to my faith.

Our church thrived on volunteerism and service. In many cases, a volunteer might have fallen short in skill, but they made up for it with zeal. One dear and faithful soul that God used to shape my faith in Christ was my elementary Sunday school teacher, Miss Theodora Lewis. To my recollection, Miss Lewis was always elderly. She lived alone. The only family I remember her ever having was church family. As far as I know, she never married or had children. Her wardrobe was never fashionable but simple and quaint. I don't remember her hair ever being styled by a professional beautician. The tufts of her naturally textured hair looked like white cotton balls that were rolled here and bobby-pinned there. She wasn't the best teacher either. With typical elementary school kids, our class always seemed to be one step from total chaos. But Miss Lewis always rolled with the punches. I thought she might eventually be replaced by a more able-bodied person, but she always held her post. She also sang in the choir. Well, she didn't actually sing—she kind of bellowed in long, indistinguishable tones. It was obvious to the choir (and to everyone else) that Miss Lewis was tone-deaf and couldn't carry a tune in a bucket.

But every Sunday, she was present and accounted for. After Sunday school adjourned, she donned her choir robe and took her place in the choir where she supported the bass section from the back row. To some, Miss Lewis was overlooked and ordinary. Her contribution seemed nominal at best. There was, however, a certain quality Miss Lewis had that distinguished her from many. Miss Lewis was faithful. Up until her death, I don't remember a church service without her in attendance. She lived a few blocks from the church. Like the proverbial postman, "neither rain, nor snow, nor sleet, nor hail" could keep Miss Lewis from her duty, which was getting to the house of God. One day in Sunday school, Miss Lewis gave every child in the class a small gift. It was a pencil with an eraser at both ends. Printed on the pencil were these words: "Life without Jesus is like this pencil. It has no point."

I may have been a better singer, but when it came to service, Miss Lewis was in a class all by herself. It was her witness, and the witness of others like her, that made the

Christian life desirable for me. I wanted to shine for Jesus the way they shined. Many members didn't have more than a high school education, but they served God and the church with ease and grace. They witnessed with boldness and persuaded people to give their lives to Christ. No doubt about it; I am a product of their faith.

The people in my father's church impacted my life in remarkable ways. It wasn't always what they said that made the biggest impression on my young faith. A lot of times, what they didn't say made the difference. It was how they lived their lives. And the thing about it is, they didn't always know I was watching them, but I was. They had no idea I was taking mental notes about them. They didn't know that the seeds they planted in my life would bear fruit that would be accounted to them.

What about you? How old were you when the gospel you knew in your head first connected with your heart? Whom did you consider a major Christian in your life? And what did you see in that person that made you want to serve Jesus? Who shared the message of salvation with you? Whose face would you carve on your Mount Rushmore? A family member? A Sunday school teacher? A coach? No matter how humble, no one is insignificant if they have impacted your faith in Christ.

Here's another way to look at it. Who's taking mental notes on you? Who, in their mind, has placed your face on their Mount Rushmore? Sobering, isn't it? Let the life you live speak for you. Evangelist and author Charles Spurgeon said it best: "A good character is the best tombstone. Those who loved you, and were helped by you, will remember you when forget-me-nots are withered. Carve your name on hearts, not on marble."[1]

The reward is not given to the fastest or the strongest—but to the one who endures. Don't be concerned with competing or comparing your life to someone else. That is a sure way to get distracted and lag behind. You won't win the race by focusing on the finish line. The race is won by focusing on Jesus. Therefore, run your own race. That should be your way of life from the moment you were saved right up till now. That is what James 1:12 tells us: "Blessed is the one who perseveres under trial because, having stood the test, that person will receive the crown of life that the Lord has promised to those who love Him" (NIV). So how would you assess the condition of your faith? Who can say that their faith is stronger because of your influence?

> # The reward is not given to the fastest or the strongest—but to the one who endures.

In this chapter, we'll talk about the importance of your Christian witness. You may be a teacher, shining your light in the classroom. You may be a flight attendant, representing Christ as you serve others at thirty-four thousand feet above the earth. You might be in the medical field, helping people with physical or emotional challenges. Or you may be a stay-at-home mom, raising up the next generation of strong believers in Christ. Regardless of where and how you shine, this is not the time to diminish your light but to turn up your light so others can see the life you are living for Jesus.

Making a World of Difference

All over the world, God is raising up people who are willing to shine their light in some of the darkest places on the earth. As millions come to Christ in the developing countries of Africa, Asia, the Middle East, Latin America, and other parts of the world, missionaries and the new believers they are bringing to Christ are placed in immediate danger for their beliefs. Some are experiencing great persecution, discrimination, torture, and even death. The good news is that in spite of living in imminent danger and persecution, people are coming to Christ exponentially from people groups across the globe. Christian churches are being established all over the world, and the gospel is being preached in nearly every language of the earth.

Maybe you have already had an opportunity to serve as a missionary and go to other places near your home or on foreign soil. If you have, then let me say thank you for being obedient to the call to shine for Christ. Over the years, Charles and I have been blessed to travel to many countries to serve as short-term missionaries. It is a humbling yet exhilarating experience to share the gospel and see people come to know Jesus. (If you have the honor of leading someone to Christ, consider having them read the prayer I wrote in the "Prayer of Salvation and Memory Verses" chapter.)

Maybe you've never had the opportunity to serve as a missionary or travel with a team on a short-term mission project. And maybe you're in a life situation where traveling is out of the picture. You can still play an important role by supporting those who do. As it's been said, "You can be a goer or you can be a sender." When you go or when you send, you are doing the work of Jesus by helping promote the gospel around the world.

Either way, we may never get to hear how the work we do for Christ bears fruit for the kingdom of God. In other chapters of this book, I've shared stories about how God has used songs I've written to minister to people in the most incredible ways. Here's another amazing story of how God used one of my songs as a teaching tool to share Christ with others.

All It Takes Is a Song

Over the years, I've had many occasions to be a guest singer at the Brooklyn Tabernacle. From the heart of New York City, Pastor Jim Cymbala leads a thriving multiethnic congregation of people from all walks of life. I have had some of the greatest joys of my life while singing with the Brooklyn Tabernacle Choir under the direction of Carol Cymbala, Pastor Jim's wife. The choir, with more than three hundred voices, and the congregation, with more than ten thousand members, sound like heaven as they worship in song together each week.

Not long ago I received a personal phone call from Pastor Cymbala. Let me tell you, it's not every day I have that privilege. So, trust me, I was all ears. He told me the story of how God is using people from his church who are willing to shine their lights in dark places. Here's the story in Pastor Cymbala's own words:[2]

Recently I heard a story that made my heart jump for joy.

One day a report came from our mission pastor, Pastor Park. He had just returned from a trip to the Middle East, where a number of Christian ministries are working to spread the gospel in a Muslim area there. The missionaries Pastor Park had visited, however, were not working with Muslims. Neither were they reaching out to the Kurds, another ethnic group in the area. Instead, they were interacting with a people group that is greatly despised by both Muslims and Kurds. This particular people group is considered the scum of the earth to other communities over there. They are considered outcasts. They are far too often victims of violence, and their families are often ravaged and torn apart by civil war. Pastor Park observed that while teaching the people simple and basic English-speaking skills, the missionaries also work their hardest to build acceptance and friendship and to establish a safe and relaxed atmosphere with this people group so that they can eventually share the gospel with them.

The missionaries realized that these people liked music, so they taught them some songs in English that might be easy for the people to learn. They thought that as they sang, maybe the people might ask questions about the messages in the songs they are learning, and that might lead to more direct witnessing. One song the mission team was teaching this group of people caught Pastor Park's attention. He told us, "I was so surprised when I heard the workers teaching the people some words to a song I recognized. 'Love is patient; love is kind; love is humble all the time.'"[3]

Oh my goodness, Pastor Park thought. *I know that song. That is a Babbie Mason song!*

Years ago, our friend Babbie Mason had come to the Brooklyn Tabernacle on a Sunday afternoon to sing and minister. She had written a new song, and she wanted to teach it to us. She began to sing, "Love is patient, love is kind; love is humble all the time. Not easily angered, enduring the test. So never forget. Love is the more excellent way." We sang Babbie's new song that day, and we have continued to sing it after Babbie left. Now, decades later, because of Pastor Park's ministry, people are singing that song in an undisclosed location in the Middle East to a people group who desperately need the love of the Lord.

I called Babbie. "Is this not amazing?" I asked, getting emotional as I spoke. "People who need Jesus are singing 'Love is patient, love is kind; love is humble all the time.'"

As people learn the song, they are compelled to ask questions like, "What kind of love is this?" "Who loves like that?" and "How do we experience this kind of love?"

So many people in the world today don't experience love. They have no idea what God's love is all about. But over in the Middle East, among a people group that needs to be reached with the gospel of Jesus Christ, God is using Babbie Mason's song "Love Is the More Excellent Way" to open a door into people's hearts. Sometimes all it takes is a song to shine the light of Christ.

My eyes filled with tears as I heard Pastor Cymbala tell me the story of how God used that simple song with a profound message as a teaching tool to share His love. I wrote the song "Love Is the More Excellent Way" with my dear friend Turner Lawton in 1996, and I recorded it on my *Heritage of Faith* record that same year. The song is a great paraphrase of 1 Corinthians 13, otherwise known as "the love chapter." Obviously, that was many years ago. But time has no boundaries in God's economy. We have no idea how or when the seeds we plant today will bear fruit down the road. But we can be positive that, in due season, they will. Can you see that, behind the scenes, God wills and works in ways we cannot even imagine? I always pray that God would use my songs however He wills. But never could I have imagined that God would use this song as a witnessing tool to teach men and women in a dark, war-torn country about the love of Christ.

Sharing the gospel doesn't always begin with the words you say. Your actions play an important role too. Pastor Cymbala expressed that living the gospel out loud is a way of spreading the good news as much as preaching it. Pastor Park and the missionaries on the field in the Middle East know that they live in a world where others are not always receptive to conversations about Jesus. Sharing the gospel may even put lives in danger because talking about the love of Christ is illegal in many parts of the Middle East. Most people, regardless of culture, respond positively to the message of Christ when it is expressed with genuine love and concern. As Pastor

Cymbala shared, demonstrating the love of Jesus can be a powerful witnessing tool. It's true: People can hear what you have to say, but they will respond more readily when you back up your words with actions.

In what ways can you show genuine concern for the needs of others? We can educate children and adults, teaching them to read and write. We can teach practical life skills in fields like homemaking, childcare, and agriculture. We can serve the poor and the outcast by providing housing, food, and clothing. Then, later on, when trust is established, our public actions can lead to private conversations where we can address the personal concerns of those in need. You'll find that when people are looking for a lifeline, they are much more open to hearing about Jesus.

Doing the Most by Serving the Least

My songwriter friend Kenn was a part of a group from his church that went on a short-term mission trip to South Africa. One day, their itinerary sent them off to lead a worship service at a local orphanage that housed children whose parents had been killed by civil war or the AIDS crisis.

When Kenn and his group arrived, the orphanage director met them and gave them a brief tour of the meager facilities and the sparse grounds. They noticed that the twenty kids who lived there looked tired, weak, and lethargic. Kenn asked about the children's poor condition. The director responded, "This is day three."

"Day three of what?" Kenn asked.

The dear lady explained that their food supplies had run out and the children at the orphanage hadn't eaten in three days. Food was due to arrive the next day. Shocked at what he was hearing, Kenn immediately asked his group members to donate any cash they could spare. The group members pooled their cash reserves. Some even gave sacrificially. Among them, they raised $250. Kenn went to the orphanage's director and shared, "How could we even think about leading the kids in a worship service when they haven't eaten in days? It's far more important to show them the love of Christ than it is to tell them."

Kenn and a couple of folks on their team took the director to a nearby market while others stayed behind to play with the kids. They returned with enough provisions to feed the children and stock the orphanage's cupboards for six months. Kenn and his group's response to this dire situation takes me right to Jesus' words in Matthew 25:31–40 (NLT):

> But when the Son of Man comes in his glory, and all the angels with him, then he will sit upon his glorious throne. All the nations will be gathered in his presence, and he will separate the people as a shepherd separates the sheep from the goats. He will place the sheep at his right hand and the goats at his left.
>
> Then the King will say to those on his right, "Come, you who are blessed by my Father, inherit the Kingdom prepared for you from the creation of the world. For I was hungry, and you fed me. I was thirsty, and you gave me a drink. I was a stranger, and you invited me into your home. I was naked, and you gave me clothing. I was sick, and you cared for me. I was in prison, and you visited me."
>
> Then these righteous ones will reply, "Lord, when did we ever see you hungry and feed you? Or thirsty and give you something to drink? Or a stranger and show you hospitality? Or naked and give you clothing? When did we ever see you sick or in prison and visit you?"
>
> And the King will say, "I tell you the truth, when you did it to one of the least of these my brothers and sisters, you were doing it to me!"

Can you see from these accounts and from the Scripture why it is imperative that others see God's love through your actions? Words are good, but sometimes words are not enough. There comes a moment when it's time to act.

The desire to serve others should be a lifelong quest. Let's talk more about ways you can be a better witness for Christ with your actions.

1. Deepen Your Own Relationship with Jesus

Start by working on an area that will strengthen your faith in Christ. Practice the daily discipline of spending dedicated time studying the Bible, talking to God in prayer, and nurturing your personal worship. The more you know about your faith and the deeper your experience with God is, the more genuine and impactful your witness will be.

As with any relationship, you can't tell others about someone you don't know. After spending time getting to know God through His Word, you'll begin to see how the Bible is applicable to your life. The apostle Paul encouraged the members of the church in Philippi to actively pursue spiritual growth: "Keep putting into practice all you learned and received from me—everything you heard from me and saw me doing. Then the God of peace will be with you" (Phil. 4:9 NLT). This means allowing the teachings of Christ to influence your actions, attitudes, and choices. Then you will have a greater spiritual impact on others.

The more you know about your faith and the deeper your experience with God is, the more genuine and impactful your witness will be.

2. Be Prepared to Share Your Testimony at the Appropriate Time

How do you become more comfortable with telling your God-story? Practice giving your testimony starting today; then share it as soon as you have opportunity. You've heard the adage "Practice makes perfect." Well, because your testimony is always evolving, you may not have the opportunity to memorize it entirely. But that's okay. Share it as best you can. You can rehearse certain parts of your testimony, such as how you came to know Christ as Savior. You can memorize a story about a particular time God answered your prayers. Then, when you have the opportunity, you can share what you rehearsed earlier. No one has to know you rehearsed it but you. Don't worry about having a perfect presentation. The most important part of your God-story is that it deserves to be told.

Your testimony is evidence of the things God has done for you. Your God-story can be used to encourage others in a small group or class. You can write it out and share it online. You might even want to volunteer to share some aspect of your God-story with your home church, in person or on video. When you share your testimony with others, you are being obedient to God's Word. Your story tells others that Jesus is responsible for the change that is taking place in your life. (For inspiration, see Mark 5:1–20, especially v. 20.)

3. Exercise Your Spiritual Gifts

God has given every believer unique and wonderful spiritual gifts. We are to use these gifts to serve others and share the love of Jesus with them. The Bible strongly urges us to find ways to use our spiritual gifts.

Do you have the gift of hospitality?

Are you a teacher?

Do you feel called to represent the cause of Christ in the marketplace?

Do you feel called to preach the gospel?

Do you have the gift of persuasive speech?

Do others compliment you on your leadership qualities?

Whatever your area of spiritual gifting, you should be excited about finding ways to use your gifts to make a positive impact by pointing those you influence to Christ. Gifts are bestowed on us by God. We receive them with joy; then we use them to make a difference.

The ultimate gift that's been given to us is Jesus Himself. Apart from Christ, we can do nothing, but with Christ, we can accomplish anything He calls us to do. Romans 12:6–8 (NLT) serves as a great call to follow Christ wherever He leads:

> In his grace, God has given us different gifts for doing certain things well. So if God has given you the ability to prophesy, speak out with as much faith as God has given you. If your gift is serving others, serve them well. If you are a teacher, teach well. If your gift is to encourage others, be encouraging. If it is giving, give generously. If God has given you leadership ability, take the responsibility seriously. And if you have a gift for showing kindness to others, do it gladly.

4. Depend on the Holy Spirit

Jesus commanded us to go and make disciples. He also knows we cannot win the lost without His help. He has given us the Holy Spirit to equip us to reach the lost. So rely on the guidance of the Holy Spirit as you seek to share your faith with others. Pray for wisdom in what to say. Pray for discernment as you ask the Lord to use you. Pray for boldness to speak up. Ask God for confidence to be an effective witness. Telling others about the Lord doesn't mean you force your beliefs on them; rather, through your words and actions you can show as well as tell others about the Lord. Pray for the mind of Christ on every matter. God will give you wisdom to know when to speak and when to act. Romans 12:2 tells us, "Don't copy the behavior and customs of this world, but let God transform you into a new person by changing the way you think. Then you will learn to know God's will for you, which is good and pleasing and perfect" (NLT).

Show Me How to Love

Since this chapter has featured some of the songs I've written, I thought I would close with a story behind one of my most meaningful songs. The song "Show Me How to Love" was inspired after learning a life lesson on the power of sharing my testimony.

In the early days of my ministry, I received an invitation to sing for an event in Florida. I accepted with excitement. Up to that point, I had sung only for local and statewide events, so this event was the first time Charles and I had ever flown out of state for an appearance. The hosts of the event sent a professional car service to pick us up from the airport. The driver of the long black limousine met us at the curb. He opened the door of the stretch vehicle, and Charles and I stepped inside to enjoy the air-conditioned car and an ice-cold soft drink while the driver went to retrieve our luggage. Once the driver closed the door, we elbowed each other in the ribs and exclaimed with delight, "Wow ... we could get used to this kind of treatment, couldn't we?"

The driver returned and drove us along the beautiful harbor to a hotel where luxurious accommodations awaited us. As we turned onto the property, I gazed out of the window to take in the meticulously manicured grounds and the towering hotel. Just before we rounded the last curve to reach the hotel entrance, I saw something that was grossly out of place. Nestled in the bushes under low hanging branches was a homeless man, asleep in the landscape.

My mind was confused. The juxtaposition of the man asleep on a piece of cardboard, just steps away from a beautiful hotel room, a warm shower, and room service was too much to conceive. When the limo came to a complete stop, I stepped out of the vehicle into the sweltering Florida heat. I left Charles and the limo driver to deal with the luggage, and I walked over to the area where I had seen the homeless man. Much to my surprise, he was gone. Where had he gone in those brief moments? How could the hotel staff have ushered him off the huge property without me noticing? It was as if he had vanished into thin air. Could the man have been an angel? I don't know.

The situation left me shaken. As I tried to make sense of it all, I heard a gentle admonishment from the Lord tugging my heart: "My dear daughter, you have My permission to enjoy the comforts of this life. I have given you all things to enjoy. Yet I have not called you to be comfortable but to be uncomfortable. I have called you to minister to the broken and the outcast. It is not those who are well who need a physician but those who are sick. Never seek to be served but to serve."

Not long after that, I was inspired to write the song "Show Me How to Love." Those words will serve as our prayer:

* * *

You didn't have to leave the glory of heaven
But You became a simple man
You didn't have to serve the poor and afflicted
But You touched and healed their brokenness
No greater love has been given
You became the ultimate sacrifice
Create in me the heart of a servant
Let this be my soul's desire

Chorus
Show me how to love in the true meaning of the word
Teach me to sacrifice expecting nothing in return
I want to give my life away
Becoming more like You each and every day
My words are not enough
Show me how to love[4]

There will be days when sharing Christ makes you uncomfortable. Your heart will be broken. Your hands will get dirty. You will rub shoulders with people who are less fortunate than you. You will pray for those who hurt. Your eyes will burn with tears. You will share the gospel with those who are lost. You will never be more like Jesus than on those days.

Reflections

1. Earlier in the chapter, I asked whose face you would chisel on your Mount Rushmore. Give that some more thought. Jot down why you chose that person.

2. What relationships are you building with people who don't know Jesus? If you don't have any, where in your community might you be able to develop those relationships?

3. When was the last time you shared your personal testimony?

4. Your personal testimony has three parts. Think about those three parts in relation to your life's story. What was your life like before you met Christ? What circumstances led you to accept Christ as your Savior and Lord? How has your life changed since you made that decision?

5. Who are the people in your life who have walked with Jesus for a significant amount of time? A parent or close relative? A teacher, pastor, or friend? As a faith-building exercise, consider asking them to share their personal testimony with you. Begin the conversation with the same questions you answered in question 4.

6. Have you ever volunteered to go on a short-term mission trip? If you have, spend a moment reflecting on a compelling or impactful memory.

7. Words are important. But when was the last time you were able to serve others by putting your faith into action? If you are actively involved in serving now, what do you enjoy most about the experience? If you are not actively involved in serving right now, consider why that is the case. Pray about how you can be a blessing to your church or a ministry organization near you.

Chapter 7

Doing Good

*Let your light so shine before men, that they may see **your
good works** and glorify your Father in heaven.*

Matthew 5:16

Encouraging words are like fresh rain on dry soil. And if good words are like
fresh rain, then good works are like a downpour. Dear friend, you have something great to contribute to this world. God gave you gifts and talents for a reason. By
doing good, you carry God's light into the world through your words, thoughts, and
actions.

People around you are looking for hope to make it through their circumstances.
They're searching for the God kind of love, which assures them they are not alone.
And they are longing for joy to fill the nagging void they feel inside. Does this
mean you don't have problems of your own? Not at all. But you know in whom your
strength lies.

Where do you think they will find these virtues?

When they encounter Jesus in you!

You are the closest encounter with Jesus some people will ever experience. If
someone doesn't know Jesus, they can get a firsthand understanding of Christ's love

when they meet you. But some days we miss the mark, don't we? Personally, there are days when I'm tired, I'm selfish, I want things my way, and I'm singing that sad song that's all about "me-me-me-me-me." Far too often my own personal needs get in the way of helping others.

I'll share another story with you of how I missed an opportunity to shine my light big-time. But thank God for His grace. He is so patient with me. I didn't feel guilty or condemned. Instead, He lovingly taught me an unforgettable lesson. God used Charles to help me realize that you cannot be a bighearted person with small-minded thinking.

The Power of Generosity

Charles and I had been on the road over the weekend. Sunday morning, we were on an early flight and, as scheduled, we arrived back home at the Atlanta airport in time to get to the Sunday morning worship service at our home church. After gathering our bags in the airport baggage claim and picking up our car from the satellite parking lot, we headed toward the church.

Because of my concert schedule, it had been three Sundays since we had attended church. I was looking forward to being there. My spirit was dry, and I had left all I had to give up on the concert stage. I needed a spiritual refill. I was looking forward to the music, the sermon, and the fellowship.

One exit from where the church is located, my husband saw that we were low on gas. He decided to stop for a few dollars' worth of fuel at a nearby station. After he pumped the gas, Charles headed inside the store to pay cash. I said from the opened window of his truck, "Hurry back. The church service will be starting in a few minutes."

On his way back to the car, Charles spotted a couple of young guys who were struggling to push their vehicle up a slight incline and into the gas station parking lot.

It was pretty obvious that their car had died. One of the guys did his best to guide the car while the other young fellow struggled to push their dead, weather-beaten jalopy into the parking lot all by himself. Seeing their plight, Charles fell right in with them and helped the guys push their hooptie of a car into a parking spot. Then he came on back to the truck.

Immediately I reminded him, "Okay, good. Now let's get on up the road or we'll be late for worship." As Charles put the truck's gear into drive, he noticed that one of the young guys was struggling to find the latch to release the hood of their car. Instead of heading for the gas station exit, Charles pulled his truck right up next to their car. Before I knew it, he was climbing out of our truck and walking over to assist these two young men. In no time at all, Charles had unlatched the hood of their car and poked his head under it to assess the problem.

You have to understand that Charles is a jack-of-all-trades and a master of quite a few. He can handle basic car repairs and routine home maintenance with no problem. If we're ever stranded on a desert island, Charles is the guy we'll need to hunt down food, start a fire, fix a barbecue, and eventually get us rescued. So I knew my hopes of attending the worship service that morning were slim to none when Charles left the front of their car, headed for the rear of his truck, and came back with his toolbox in tow.

Those two young guys knew immediately that they were in good hands. I saw them put their hands in their pockets and lean up against the store window to escape the brunt of the chilly weather. I, on the other hand, was growing hot around the collar as I stewed in my seat inside the truck. I watched the minutes tick away, and I knew we were going to miss the worship service altogether. I grew more perturbed because I knew, due to a busy concert schedule, it would be another couple of weeks before we could make it to a worship service.

Twenty or thirty minutes went by, and Charles instructed one of the guys to hop into their car and see if it would start. Deep in my heart, I knew it would. I have that much confidence in my husband's mechanical skills. I saw the young guy motion as he patted the accelerator, and I heard the car cough and sputter. Sure enough, the car's motor turned over.

I glanced over in time to catch the expression of the young fellow who sat behind the wheel. His face lit up like a sunbeam as he gunned the car's motor. His bright eyes connected with mine. It was then that I saw his familiar facial features. Beautiful brown skin, high cheekbones, and almond-shaped eyes led me to surmise that these two young men were probably from East Africa, maybe Kenya or Uganda. That's probably why my husband stopped to help them. He recognized those features too.

We have been on a number of mission trips to Kenya and Uganda where I have sung in concerts and Charles has helped to dig wells and build churches and schools. We have many friends there and lots of memories of the great work God is doing in that part of the world. When I made that connection in my mind, I quickly wondered about their story. What brought these young men to the States? Were they students? Refugees? Where were their parents? Alive and living in the Atlanta area or dead as victims of civil war? If their parents were alive and knew they were stranded, could their mother be praying for them at that very moment, that if her sons were stranded, a kind, caring, and compassionate man like Charles would come along and rescue them?

When that thought settled in my heart, the floodgates opened up and the tears began to flow from my eyes. It hit me like a ton of bricks. While I couldn't wait to go to church to hear about the light, Charles was *being* the light to the world around him. While I was concerned about getting to church, Charles was *being* the church. My husband was preaching the sermon of a lifetime right before my eyes. By his good works, Charles was preaching a sermon without stepping foot onto a platform or raising a microphone or receiving a love offering. As Charles was giving the young men some final instructions, I sat in the front seat of the truck and prayed. My first prayer was, "Lord, thank You for my husband, Charles Mason. Bless him as he shines for You." My second prayer was, "God, strengthen *me* to be a better servant."

God used Charles to teach me a great lesson: we can make the gospel attractive by the generous things we do for others. It's easy to say we love God; anyone can do that. But Jesus makes it clear that it's every believer's responsibility to actively love our neighbor—particularly those who fall on hard times. By now you probably know I enjoy character studies. In this chapter, let's observe the Good Samaritan and the good works of his generous heart, hardworking hands, and levelheaded thinking. When we engage with all that God has given us, we can push back the power of darkness with love and generous living.

The Good Samaritan

On one occasion, Jesus was teaching on the subject of loving one's neighbor. In this account, as with the woman caught in adultery, you'll find religious leaders attempting to test Jesus with tricky questions. As spiritual guides and teachers of the law, the Pharisees were supposed to be the moral example in the community. They failed miserably when Jesus put their efforts to shame by exposing their blatant hypocrisy and inconsistencies. Here, Jesus told the story of the Good Samaritan in Luke 10:25–37 (NLT). Read the account now.

> One day an expert in religious law stood up to test Jesus by asking him this question: "Teacher, what should I do to inherit eternal life?"
>
> Jesus replied, "What does the law of Moses say? How do you read it?"
>
> The man answered, "'You must love the LORD your God with all your heart, all your soul, all your strength, and all your mind.' And, 'Love your neighbor as yourself.'"

"Right!" Jesus told him. "Do this and you will live!"

The man wanted to justify his actions, so he asked Jesus, "And who is my neighbor?"

Jesus replied with a story: "A Jewish man was traveling from Jerusalem down to Jericho, and he was attacked by bandits. They stripped him of his clothes, beat him up, and left him half dead beside the road.

"By chance a priest came along. But when he saw the man lying there, he crossed to the other side of the road and passed him by. A Temple assistant walked over and looked at him lying there, but he also passed by on the other side.

"Then a despised Samaritan came along, and when he saw the man, he felt compassion for him. Going over to him, the Samaritan soothed his wounds with olive oil and wine and bandaged them. Then he put the man on his own donkey and took him to an inn, where he took care of him. The next day he handed the innkeeper two silver coins, telling him, 'Take care of this man. If his bill runs higher than this, I'll pay you the next time I'm here.'

"Now which of these three would you say was a neighbor to the man who was attacked by bandits?" Jesus asked.

The man replied, "The one who showed him mercy."

Then Jesus said, "Yes, now go and do the same."

Loving with All Your Heart

As Jesus was teaching on what it looks like to love one's neighbor, a lawyer asked Jesus the self-justifying question, "Who is my neighbor?" This lawyer had no desire to learn or grow in his faith; he only wanted to justify his own selfish behavior. Even today, some so-called Christians are like that. They have no interest in shining a light, only throwing shade on those who want to do good. In Luke 10 we see religious people who have no dealings with others who are not like them. In fact, religious people—a priest and a temple assistant—crossed over to the other side of the road to avoid assisting the man who was beaten by robbers. They had no desire to love God or love others, let alone love people who did not share their views and values.

When the Samaritan man found the beaten stranger on the roadside, his first response was to have compassion and pity for the dying man. That is the response of Jesus. Whether it's Black people or white people, Jews or Arabs, rich or poor, Jesus wants us to see each other as neighbors. With a heart full of sympathy for the man's plight and a true expression of love for his fellow man, the Good Samaritan cared for a perfect stranger and looked after all his needs.

Loving with All Your Strength

When the Samaritan came upon the half-dead man who had been lying alongside the dusty road, he sprang into action and provided immediate help. He tended to the man's wounds, which were many, and cleaned and bandaged him up. Then the Samaritan loaded the man on his own beast. It's possible the Samaritan man had to walk the remaining distance into the nearby town, maybe even removing some of his personal items and carrying some of the load himself. In addition to renting a room, he charged the innkeeper with the responsibility to provide a comfortable bed, food, bandages, and whatever else was necessary to aid in the wounded man's recovery. Then he promised to foot the entire bill upon his return to the town. This may indicate the Samaritan was a regular working-class guy with limited resources. But he used the means he had to see after a stranger who had fallen into the hands of thieves. What he couldn't pay up front, he was willing to work hard to raise the extra money for the stranger's care. Giving the innkeeper his word, he would pay the balance upon his return.

Many people wouldn't dare to do all this for someone they know. But the Samaritan was willing to do all this for a man he had never met. Caring for others is hard work. Loving one another may mean putting in long hours of hard work, getting our hands dirty, going out of our way, or contributing our financial resources. Jesus never hesitates to go out of His way to come to our aid. We should be ready to do the same.

Loving with All Your Mind

One big problem the religious leaders in this story had was a closed mind. The priest and temple assistant demonstrated self-righteous behavior, believing their own pious religiosity was enough to save them. In this instance, *religiosity* is another word for *hypocrisy*. Not wanting to get their hands dirty, so to speak, they avoided getting involved. I'm sure you've heard people say these words: "Well, I thought about it, but I didn't want to get involved."

Thank God, when we get saved, our minds get saved too. That means when we give our lives to Christ, we also present our minds to Him to be completely renewed. It's necessary for the mind to be regenerated so we can say instead, "It's going to be messy, but I need to look out for my neighbor." Without regeneration, there is no way we can love God or serve others. As we grow in Him, we are, as the apostle Paul says in Romans 12:2, "transformed by the renewing of [our] mind." When we love Jesus with all our mind, we honor Him and hold Him in high esteem. We meditate on His goodness with reverence and adoration.

But let's face it, everyone we encounter won't be receptive to the Christlike attitude we hope to convey. Some people were resistant to Jesus. Others disagreed with Him. But that didn't keep Him from touching people's lives right where they lived. Please don't allow resistance from others to discourage you. In my experience, those who respond positively to good deeds far outnumber those who do not. The light you shine will be the light you get back in return.

Everything Changes

Don't forget this, beloved: You are not blessed because you are good. You are blessed because God is good to you. Out of the overflow of those countless blessings, good works are generated. Good works are an outward expression of an inner relationship. American author and poet Albert Pike said this: "What we have done for ourselves alone, dies with us; what we have done for others and the world, remains and is immortal."[1] In other words, every good deed goes a long, long way. We can all appreciate generosity, particularly if we are the one in need. It's never too late to begin practicing this virtue. Our lives are much richer all because someone blessed us through an act of giving. Jesus challenges us to practice generosity because it reflects God's character and draws people to the light of Christ.

You are not blessed because you are good. You are blessed because God is good to you.

Have you ever walked into a darkened room in your home and flipped on the light switch, but the light didn't come on? When that happens to me, I automatically assume that something is wrong. *Is there a power failure somewhere? Is there a disconnected circuit? Is the light bulb blown? Did I pay the power bill?*

The same is true spiritually. If you say you are a Christian but your life doesn't produce light, something is wrong somewhere. There is a disconnect along the line. We can draw a simple principle from this illustration: in the presence of light, darkness will always disappear. When someone who has walked in darkness receives Christ, their life will produce light. Jesus Himself said, "I have come into the world as light, so that whoever believes in me may not remain in darkness" (John 12:46 ESV). Good works are evidence to a dark world that the light of Christ lives inside of you.

Good Works for the Right Reason

Doing good communicates you are on the Lord's side. You are taking time to study God's Word through this book, and that indicates you don't want an average, mediocre faith, but you want to live a life that is pleasing to God in every way—a life full of good works.

When you make the study of God's Word a priority, you are working on the inside, where you have all the fruit of the Spirit. Loving difficult people becomes easier with the Holy Spirit's help. You have joy even when your heart is saddened. You can find peace in the midst of chaos. In situations where you'd normally be short-tempered or irritated, you find that God has given you more patience. You look forward to being kind to others. You really want to be good to your family and friends. You have a renewed desire to be faithful in your relationships. You are more conscious of your words and actions. You depend on the Holy Spirit for self-control.

All that faith building on the inside will burst forth on the outside through good works. What does James 2:26 say? "Faith without works is dead." Or, put it another way, "God does not need your good works, but your neighbor does."[2] Genuine faith always produces good works.

Abiding in Christ

Have you ever practiced the piano? Learned a foreign language? Rehearsed a speech? What you were doing was mentally preparing yourself for a future performance.

Now think about that in spiritual terms. When you practice the spiritual disciplines of spending meaningful time with God, praying to Him, reading His Word, memorizing Scripture, prioritizing solitude, and giving thanks, you are doing what the Bible calls "abiding" in Him. God wants your life to become deeply rooted, grounded, and established in Him.

When you abide in Christ, spiritually speaking, you make a decision, pick the perfect spot to settle down, and stay awhile. It sounds simple, but you must "decide to abide." The word *abide* is a verb that means to "remain," "live," or "wait for."[3] Spiritual maturity doesn't happen overnight. To live a fruitful life—one that looks like Jesus' life—you must spend time with Him. Here are His words put plainly in John 15:4–6:

> Abide in Me, and I in you. As the branch cannot bear fruit of itself, unless it abides in the vine, neither can you, unless you abide in Me.
>
> I am the vine, you are the branches. He who abides in Me, and I in him, bears much fruit; for without Me you can do nothing. If anyone does not abide in Me, he is cast out as a branch and is withered; and they gather them and throw them into the fire, and they are burned.

The passage tells us that a branch cannot bear fruit unless it abides in the vine. And verses 5–6 tell us that if we abide in the vine—which is Christ—we will bear much fruit. And if He does not live in us, we will not bear any fruit at all but will be like dead branches that are good for nothing but kindling for a blazing bonfire.

Here in Georgia, we have tall, stately pine trees. Several species of pine tree can grow as tall as 150 feet. They are typically strong and resilient. But during heavy rain, strong winds, icy weather, or winter snow, the Georgia pine tree's branches can break easily under the weight of adverse conditions. If the soil around the tree's root system becomes waterlogged, the tree's roots can become weak, causing the tree to uproot and fall.

On the other hand, in the state of Florida, our neighbor to the south, you'll find the palm tree standing strong and tall after fires, floods, freezes, and hurricane winds. Its root system wraps itself around the earth, and its flexible trunk allows it to bend almost level to the ground in the fiercest storms. In fact, the sabal palm can endure hurricane-force winds up to 145 miles per hour.[4]

The Lord wants you to be like the palm tree, so rooted, so grounded in Him that the storms and adverse circumstances of life won't cause you to break under the pressure. When we abide in Christ, a life full of immense joy that overflows with good works is the result.

The Sweet Life

Let me tell you more about Charles. He grew up on a farm in rural Alabama. He loves the out of doors, and he enjoys raising vegetables in his summer and fall gardens. He enjoys doing what I call "playing in the dirt." Charles has a muscadine vineyard on the small farm where we live. A muscadine is like a super grape. The fleshy fruit on the inside is sumptuous and hearty, and even the skin of the fruit has many healthy properties.

Each spring after the winter weather breaks, I can find Charles out in the vineyard, pruning the vines. Regular pruning is necessary to produce high fruit yields. Removing old, dead growth, Charles prunes the muscadine vines so they will produce a bumper crop in late summer. During the process, Charles can prune the vines so severely I think he's going to damage them or even kill them. He always says, "Just wait and see." And he is right! In late August when the fruit is harvested, it is so plentiful that the vines are laden with an overabundance of fruit. And the muscadine fruit is so sweet, it tastes like candy. So it is in the life of the believer. Again, verses from John's gospel summarize this reality: "Every branch that bears fruit He prunes, that it may bear more fruit" (15:2).

Just as trees and shrubs need to be pruned from time to time, we need to be pruned at different seasons in our lives. Maybe there are areas where "dead branches" weigh you down and don't produce any fruit at all. Are there places in your life that are overgrown or out of control? No one enjoys the process of pruning. It's uncomfortable and maybe even painful. But it's a good thing to take an honest look at our lives, then ask God to show us those areas that are hindering us from growing in our relationship with Him. In fact, those dead places actually steal health and vitality from areas that already bear fruit. Jesus, the master gardener, looks at our lives and determines that we could be much more fruitful in one area or another. He is the true vine.

God prunes the life of every believer because He loves us. He does not prune us because He is angry with us. Nor does He prune us to punish us or discourage us. God prunes us because when the pruning process is done, we will bear more fruit for His glory.

Being honest with God might make you feel a bit vulnerable. The good thing is that you can be completely honest and open with God. He knows everything about you, yet He loves you. So start your prayer conversation with God by asking this simple question: "God, what dead weight am I carrying around that is hindering me from growing closer to You? What old wounds or dead relationships from the past are causing my life to be stuck or out of balance? What brings on fear and anxiety? What steps can I take to inspire new and healthy growth?"

Granted, there is nothing fun about being pruned. You'll discover that the pain of pruning is short-lived compared to the lifelong pain of holding on to unforgiveness, jealousy, and anger. Trust God, dear friend. Relinquish the stranglehold you have on your painful circumstances, and let it go. You can trust God during the pruning process. He does not want to harm you; God is cutting away dead areas of your life to make room for more. The fruit of your life will be richer and sweeter. The result is a life that can give God greater honor and glory.

Good Works for the Right Season

The second reason good works are important is because we will reap what we sow. Every Christian should get excited about doing good because, in due season, we will reap huge blessings from God. It's a lot like going to the bank. You get out of it what you put into it. Actually, if your money is invested properly, you'll get more out than what you put in. That's the way God's kingdom operates. You cannot out-give God. He keeps on giving and giving and giving. People who don't really know God's character may think God is stingy and miserly. They may have been taught that God is holding out on us or that He doesn't want to bless us. But that, my friend, is not true of the God we serve. He wants to bless us. His desire is to lavish us with His goodness. The word *lavish* means "sumptuously rich, elaborate, or luxurious."[5] Now putting that into context, read 1 John 3:1: "See what great love the Father has lavished on us, that we should be called children of God! And that is what we are!" (NIV). When we know we are loved, we can live a hope-filled life and love those around us with lavish generosity.

Besides tending to his muscadine vineyard, Charles plants a big garden every spring. He plants rows of "taters" and "maters," beans and greens. There is nothing better than fresh vegetables from the garden. Every year, I marvel at how seeds go into the soil and a harvest comes out. Charles calls the process "a God thing."

It *is* a God thing! My mind is blown away by the fact that one kernel of corn can be planted into the ground and produce an entire stalk of corn. Depending on the type of corn, on average, one stalk will produce four to six ears of corn. And each ear of corn has about eighteen to twenty-four rows of corn—or about 800 kernels.[6] The same reproduction process is true of green beans, tomatoes, squash, melons, and grapes. One tomato seed grows a bush that will produce eighteen to twenty tomatoes. When one pecan is planted, it grows a tree, producing 200 to 250 pounds of pecans. One hog produces a litter of ten to twelve piglets. In the same light, you always reap much more than you sow. Now that is some kind of reproduction system!

The same is true of good works. It's a God thing too. Good seed must fall on needy soil. And when it does, the impact of your good work goes a long, long way with lasting results.

Look around you. Do you see people who are hungry, lonely, sick, or without hope? I guarantee you, wherever you are right now, you are not far from an opportunity to do good. When a good deed is performed in the name of Christ, the blessing is multiplied. That is why Proverbs 11:25 says, "A generous person will prosper; whoever refreshes others will be refreshed" (NIV).

You cannot out-give God. He keeps on giving and giving and giving.

When you bless others, three things always happen. It's like a threefold cord. First, your heart receives an abundance of encouragement. Then the recipient is blessed by your generosity. And when it's all said and done, God receives the glory. That threefold cord equation is enough to encourage you to continue being a blessing.

It's not up to us to decide who is on the receiving end of our good works. That's God's business. We do good works because, when we do, heaven has a way of multiplying our efforts, causing us to bear fruit that has eternal value. Our good works will result in a blessing to others. The implication is simple: If you want to be blessed, be a blessing.

Good Works Last

Many people perform good works because they think it will earn them favor with God. They believe that if they work a little harder, pray a little longer, pay a little more money, serve on a committee at church, if they're good enough, then they can earn salvation. This just is not true. The Bible tells us in Romans 3:23 that "all have sinned and fall short of the glory of God." Isaiah 64:6 reminds us that when we think we are at our best, we are still at our worst: "We are all infected and impure with sin. When we display our righteous deeds, they are nothing but filthy rags" (NLT).

Yes, you will be blessed here in this life. But living for this life is empty and temporary. Think about it: Everything we buy or accumulate in this world eventually grows old, loses its value, goes out of style, gets rusty, or corrodes. Sooner or later, it will deteriorate to a worthless pile of rubble. I know it's a sobering thought, but after you die, a few pieces of your clothing, a purse or two, a stack of your books, and a few trinkets will be distributed among your family members. The rest, I'm sorry to say, will be donated or discarded.

The Bible challenges us not to lay up for ourselves treasures on earth but to lay up treasures in heaven (Matt. 6:19). You know you can't take things with you to heaven. Why would you want to, anyway? It will all pale in comparison to the glory of God's holiness and splendor. But we can take trophies of grace with us to heaven. Those are the people we told about Jesus—the lives that came to Christ because of our influence. The years of faithful service to your church or the money you contribute toward the work of ministry will not be offered in vain.

We will receive the reward for the work we did in this life. But we won't collect crowns and rewards to pat ourselves on the back. Every crown or commendation we receive is one we will gladly lay at the feet of Jesus in worship to Him. Think of it as a commencement day for the believer. As the Bible says, "For we must all appear before the judgment seat of Christ, so that each of us may receive what is due us for the things done while in the body, whether good or bad" (2 Cor. 5:10 NIV).

Have you done some evaluating of your own life? I don't know about you, but I hope to stand before God at the end of this earthly life with no assignment undone, having used everything He gave me. I want to hear Him say, "Well done, good and faithful servant. You have been faithful over a little; I will set you over much. Enter into the joy of your master" (Matt. 25:23 ESV). We find this verse in the parable of the talents. In the story, two servants were faithful in doing what their master had asked of them, and one was not. The work that the two successful servants did for the master proved to be worthwhile. As a result, the master rewarded them with high commendations and the promise that they would do much greater works. In this parable, the master is Jesus Christ, Himself. Who are the faithful servants in the story? They are you, me, and every Christian who desires to do good works for the kingdom.

The best thing you can do with your life is live it to the maximum for Jesus. Remember my mantra: Everything you do for Christ matters—and lasts. After salvation, the most incredible thing you can do is shine your light so others can see Christ in you. You may be the only Christian in your family. Don't slack off. Don't slow down or ease up. Continue to be a witness to those in your house. You might be the only Christian on your job. Don't grow weary of shining your light around your coworkers. Remain faithful to Christ. If you are a young single adult and all your friends have abandoned you because you don't participate in drinking or doing drugs, don't compromise your integrity. You have a friend in Jesus. He is the best friend you'll ever have!

Your godly influence may seem small. But as we just discussed, even small seeds can yield a great harvest. Don't give up on doing what is right in the eyes of God. Don't give in to discouragement and compromise your integrity. Press through to higher heights and deeper depths. Yielding even an inch of your territory to your spiritual adversary is not an option. The enemy of your soul only wants to thwart your efforts and destroy your testimony. You've got a reward coming! It may look as if you are fighting a losing battle but, when all is said and done, God promises that you will win in the end. You will be rewarded for the people you led to the Lord. You will be commended for how well you served here on the earth. So don't give up now! You've come too far to turn around. There's too much at stake.

Here's the bottom line. People can't see the faith you have in Christ. Your faith is experienced way deep down on the inside. But people can see the *evidence* of your faith through your good works that are demonstrated on the outside. They can see how you treat others with respect. People can observe how you show kindness to those you work with. People can see how you respond when you are treated unfairly. What they see is the fruit of your faith, or your good works. We are not saved by good works. We are saved *for* good works. While good works cannot save us, we can commit to being used by God because we love Him. Don't worry about the size of the work. We all want to do great things for God. In God's eyes, however, even the smallest effort of generosity, produced with great passion, will reap an eternal reward. Mother Teresa said, "Be faithful in small things because it is in them that your strength lies."[7] I want to do all that I can, to be a person of generosity.

Will you join me in expressing God's love through the generous work of your hands, your compassionate heart, and your wise thinking? Never forget: Love isn't love until you give it away. There's so much to think about concerning this chapter. Could we pray together and ask God to help us have a heart like His?

Dear Father, today's message really hits home. The world we live in is so "me" focused. People can be cold, insensitive, and even careless. I admit, God, that sometimes I fall right into that mindset as I think about my own little world. Help me to be a "Good Samaritan" to those who are hurting, who are forgotten, or who may just need a kind word to lift them up. In Your strength, I can do this. In Christ's name, amen.

Reflections

1. What kind of person might need to hear the story of the Good Samaritan?

2. What are people like who love God with the works of their hands, a compassionate heart, and levelheaded wisdom?

3. How would you apply the story of the Good Samaritan to your own life?

4. Knowing that Jesus is the master gardener, what would pruning look like in your life?

5. What might be the cause of your resistance to God's pruning in your life? Fear? A lack of trust? Pride? Examine your heart and ask God to help you surrender these areas to Him.

6. What places in your life are unfruitful or out of balance? What first step can you take to begin getting life back into a place of balance?

7. What would experiencing a more fruitful life look like for you?

8. Take an honest look at your daily routine. In what areas have you developed careless and harmful habits? Will you take a few moments to submit those areas to God now?

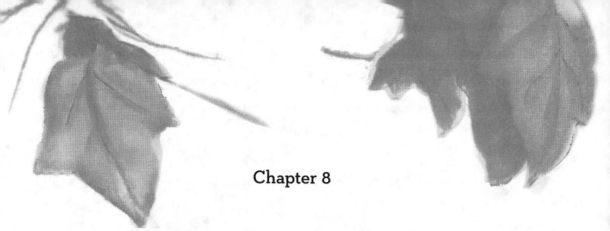

Chapter 8

Making God Look Good

Let your light so shine before men,
that they may see your good works and
glorify your Father in heaven.

Matthew 5:16

When you're a kid on a family road trip, eye-opening discoveries abound. When I was around eight years old, my dad took my younger sister, Benita, and me to visit our grandparents. The ride to Detroit took a little over an hour. Around the halfway point, we rode through the college town of Ann Arbor.

Off to the south side of the road there is an old cemetery. The graveyard is covered with big tombstones and sits in the shadows of huge evergreen trees. As we passed it, Dad asked us a question: "Girls, how many people do you think are dead over there in that cemetery?"

Benita took a wild guess. "I think there are about three hundred people dead over there in that cemetery."

I responded in protest. "No, that cemetery is huge! There has to be at least four hundred fifty or even five hundred that are dead over there!"

My sister and I were still at an age when we believed our parents knew just about everything. So, we asked, "Okay, Dad. How many people are dead over there in the cemetery?"

Dad responded with a chuckle, in his commonsensical way, "All of them!"

Created on Purpose

I still get a giggle from the dad joke we shared that day. But that light and comedic moment left a great impression on me. Now when I pass a cemetery, I often wonder about the people buried in their graves. How many of them knew the Lord Jesus as Savior? Had they fulfilled their God-given destiny? What had they done to honor God with their lives?

"Why am I here?" and "What is my purpose in life?" Those are the questions most of us will ask at some point in our lives. Fear and anxiety will paralyze some as they question their future. Some will be struck by a divorce, an illness, a career change, or the death of a loved one. Depression or loneliness will stall others. And many will become a sad statistic because of an addiction to drugs or alcohol.

Do you question the reason *you* were born? You may think you are here on planet earth to live a successful life. That is a commendable aim, but that is not the reason you were born. You may think you were created to accumulate wealth, acquire fame, and make a name for yourself. Those can be worthy goals, but they don't define your existence. You may want to make your parents proud and carry on your family's legacy. As good as that sounds, that is not the reason God placed you here.

While all those things are good, none of them explain why you were born. For the resolution to that question—and all of life's questions—the Bible has the answers. In Revelation 4:11 you will discover the meaning of your purpose: "Thou art worthy, O Lord, to receive glory and honour and power: for thou hast created all things, and for thy pleasure they are and were created" (KJV).

The answer to your existence begins and ends with a holy God who is worthy of worship. The word *worship* means to "give homage," "reverence," or "honor" to someone or something.[1] When we worship something or someone, we will esteem it or treasure it higher than anything else; we will honor it as what takes the highest priority. When you treasure something in this manner, your actions follow accordingly. Therefore, worshipping God means esteeming Him higher than anyone or anything else, giving Him first place in our hearts and lives.

You can find your life's purpose only in your worship of God. Why? Because He created you to worship Him. The fact is everyone worships someone or something. It may be money, an idol, a famous sports figure, or a Hollywood entertainer. Everyone bows down at an altar. God has placed the longing to worship within us. That's what Ecclesiastes 3:11 says: "Yet God has made everything beautiful for its own time. He has planted eternity in the human heart, but even so, people cannot see the whole scope of God's work from beginning to end" (NLT). The awareness that there is something far greater than you—greater than anything you can imagine—comes from God. He orchestrated it all. Your heavenly Father designed your birth so you would be here on the earth at this precise time in history to bring Him glory with your life.

Now you can worship with the psalmist King David, who wrote: "Bless the LORD, O my soul; and all that is within me, bless His holy name! Bless the LORD, O my soul, and forget not all His benefits" (Ps. 103:1–2).

When we think of worship, many people often assume we are talking about a musical genre. While music plays an important role in the worship experience, worship is so much more than a style, a lyric, or a tempo. Music may be categorized by the term "worship music." But real worship goes way beyond style. You may sing worship music in church on Sunday, but a lifestyle of worship embraces every moment. God ordained your very existence to bring honor, glory, reverence, and pleasure to Him.

Everything you do in life can be an act of worship. The moments you spend playing with your kids can be filled with joyful thanksgiving to God. In the evening, as you perform mundane tasks such as washing dinner dishes or folding the laundry, you can spend time praying for your family. The time you spend in traffic going to and from work is the perfect setting to practice God's presence by memorizing Scripture. Or you may want to set aside thirty minutes during your lunch hour just to be perfectly silent while enjoying fresh air, sunshine, and a few moments of solitude.

God ordained your very existence to bring honor, glory, reverence, and pleasure to Him.

Jesus often retreated to the mountains, the garden, or the lake for moments of worship, reflection, and solitude. He demonstrated the importance of establishing these habits. It's all worship when it's done intentionally to please God and bring honor to Him. How often are we supposed to do this? All day long according to Psalm 113:3, which says, "From the rising of the sun to the place where it sets, the name of the LORD is to be praised" (NIV). Practically speaking, it may not be possible to devote every single minute of the day to praying and reading your Bible. But it is possible to be aware of His presence throughout your day. A worship-driven relationship with God is what gives your life worth, meaning, and value.

You may think you are here because your parents got together and had a baby. You may have even been told that your birth was unplanned—that you are an "oops" baby. Let me confirm the truth right here: You are not a problem, an irritation, or an aggravation. You are not a mishap, an unplanned pregnancy, a mistake, or an inconvenience. You were created to enjoy your relationship with God.

Listen, dear one, you may have been a surprise to some. But you are not—nor have you ever been—a surprise to God. Your birth was on God's calendar since before creation. Regardless of the circumstances of your birth, God has always had a design and purpose for your life.

Reading the following passage will remind you that you are precious to God and He planned every day of your life:

> You made all the delicate, inner parts of my body
>> and knit me together in my mother's womb.
> Thank you for making me so wonderfully complex!
>> Your workmanship is marvelous—how well I know it.
> You watched me as I was being formed in utter seclusion,
>> as I was woven together in the dark of the womb.
> You saw me before I was born.
>> Every day of my life was recorded in your book.
> Every moment was laid out
>> before a single day had passed. (Ps. 139:13–16 NLT)

Before you were a gleam in your mother's eye, you were in God's mind and on His heart. God created you *on purpose* as an object of His affection. There has never been another person like you, and there will never be another one like you. Yes, when God created you, He broke the mold. You are unique, set apart, and beautiful. Everything God made is beautiful—including you.

Created with a Purpose

How can you begin to live the life of purpose God has planned for you? Even in tough times, you can rest assured that God has a plan. Read further to understand that God is always working. God's prophet Jeremiah wrote a letter to the exiled children of Israel who were slaves in Babylon. God's chosen people were under the oppression of their enemies in a land where the people had rejected God. The Babylonians, who were notorious idol worshippers, had lived in rebellion to God's laws ever since they built the Tower of Babel to make a name for themselves (Gen. 11:1–9).

Jeremiah wrote to remind the Israelites that the Lord was with them even though they lived in enemy territory, and he encouraged those in exile to build homes in Babylon. They were to settle down, marry, have families, plant gardens, and make a life there. They were to be a light among this pagan nation and influence the culture. Jeremiah told them even to pray for the city's peace and prosperity because if their captors prospered, they would too. They were to live for God right there among their enemies. Although Jeremiah didn't write his words *to* us, they were certainly written *for* us. God reminds us that even amid trying circumstances, He has a plan that is working on our behalf. The Lord spoke through the prophet Jeremiah to hearten the exiles with these famous words:

> "For I know the plans I have for you," declares the LORD, "plans to prosper you and not to harm you, plans to give you hope and a future. Then you will call on me and come and pray to me, and I will listen to you. You will seek me and find me when you seek me with all your heart." (Jer. 29:11–13 NIV)

Maybe you have questions about your challenging circumstances. You could be in a tough marriage where your husband doesn't want anything to do with God. You may have children who are in defiance to God's Word. Jeremiah 29:11–13 reminds us that no matter what we face, God has a plan. You may not see it. You may not know how it's going to work out. But you can know for sure that God is behind the scenes, orchestrating every detail.

I've named the Jeremiah passage quoted above "God's phone number" to remind me I can call on God any time of day or night. Put your personal area code in front of the numbers so you can remember. It's like this: 555-JER-2912. Let's read Jeremiah 29:12 again: "Then you will *call on me* and come and pray to me, and I will listen to you" (NIV).

God knows you have questions about your life. When you ask of God, you won't get the stiff arm or the silent treatment. When you call on God, you won't get a busy signal or a voicemail message to call back later to make an appointment. No, God invites you to inquire of Him. He says, "Call on Me." You are not here just to take up space or to bide your time until you grow old and die.

Dear friend, you are here to fulfill God's plan. Nothing is more exciting than living a life that brings glory and honor to the name of Christ. It's easy to think of your life as a lot of disconnected events. You get up in the morning. You get ready for the day. You fight traffic. You go to work for eight hours. You come home and fix something for dinner. You help the kids with their homework and do dishes. You go to bed. Then you get up the next day and do it all over again.

God created you for more than a merry-go-round of mundane events. God handpicked you to enjoy Him and to make a positive difference in your home, your work, and your community. I have found that if you ask people who has had the greatest influence in their lives, they usually won't refer to presidents, politicians, or Hollywood actors. They will almost always speak of everyday people like a parent, a teacher, or a coach—someone who considered him or herself ordinary. Even those things you consider mundane can be done with purpose.

If you consider yourself ordinary, then you fit the description of a godly influencer. You were born to make the world a better place by advancing the kingdom of

God with your ordinary, everyday life. When you realize the power of your influence, reverting to mediocrity will never again be an option. You must make the moments count.

If you feel unqualified for such a task, consider the story of one of the most influential figures in the Bible, God's prophet Moses. He led Israel out of slavery in Egypt and brought God's people to the Land of Promise. Exodus 3 is the amazing story of how God appeared as a burning bush and called Moses to be the leader of the Hebrew slaves. In that defining moment, God told Moses that He had seen the plight of His people who were in bondage in Egypt. In a place of seclusion, on the back side of the desert, God chose Moses to go before Pharaoh and tell this evil leader to let His people go (Ex. 3:1–10).

Moses's response is so familiar. Listen to what he told the Lord God:

> Moses pleaded with the LORD, "O Lord, I'm not very good with words. I never have been, and I'm not now, even though you have spoken to me. I get tongue-tied, and my words get tangled."
>
> Then the LORD asked Moses, "Who makes a person's mouth? Who decides whether people speak or do not speak, hear or do not hear, see or do not see? Is it not I, the LORD? Now go! I will be with you as you speak, and I will instruct you in what to say."
>
> But Moses again pleaded, "Lord, please! Send anyone else." (Ex. 4:10–13 NLT)

Does Moses's response sound familiar? Basically, Moses said to God, "Uh, God. Hold up a minute. I don't think so. You've got the wrong guy. I'm not the one. I'm unqualified. I stutter. I don't have what it takes to get the job done. You need to find someone else!"

But God knew what He was doing. From the very beginning, His hand was on the life of Moses, and He shaped that great man of God into the leader He wanted him to become. Read how Acts 7:22 recalls Moses: "And Moses was learned in all the wisdom of the Egyptians, and was mighty in words and deeds."

Most of us have felt as Moses did and said no to God at some time in our lives. And we've all been weak and had moments of unbelief when we have doubted God could ever use us or the gifts we have to offer. You see, the very thing that Moses could not see in himself, God saw in him. Pastor and author Chuck Swindoll makes a powerful point: "God has a beautiful way of bringing good vibrations out of broken chords."[2]

That's what God has done with my life. In 1998, I was a guest on a program at WATC TV 57, a local Christian television station in the Atlanta area. I enjoy doing radio and television interviews. I get to tell those in the audience about the great things God is doing in my life. But I never would have imagined that the television station would ask me to host my own program. Never one to shy away from a new adventure, I said yes. For twenty-five years, I have hosted a talk show called *Babbie's House*. I interview authors, singers, pastors, actors, and ordinary people with extraordinary stories. I had been interviewed many times before the show began, but suddenly I was the one asking all the questions. I was responsible for keeping the conversation upbeat, interesting, and relevant. When I first began hosting the show, I was overwhelmed by all the details, time cues, and wardrobe changes. I felt insecure, like Moses. I doubted my decision and my abilities. I was sure I was the wrong person for the job.

But in my weakness, God proved Himself strong. He is still using me in ways I never imagined. God wants to do the same thing with your life. Every experience you've ever had—the great opportunities, the awful setbacks, even the failures—has produced the person God is designing you to be. The good thing is He isn't done with you yet; He's still working on you. These collective defining moments are shaping and making you into God's woman for this hour.

If you look back on the tough times of your life, you can see how they have added meaning and beauty. (Sometimes this process takes a while, but it will happen.) God built this story arc into the human psyche. That's why every award-winning movie has a well-told but simple story. There are high points, low valleys, and lots of drama in the middle. And a great story is only as fantastic as its ending. The same is true of your life. Somehow, someway, in spite of the good and bad times, God allows your pain to find a purpose and your life to result in beauty. Romans 8:28 offers so much hope for those going through trials: "And we know that God causes everything to work together for the good of those who love God and are called according to his purpose for them" (NLT).

God created you with a distinct purpose. You have an unlimited, boundless, unrestricted supply of power that is working in you right now to carry out the purpose of God for your life. It is God who has called you, and it is God who has equipped you with everything you need. See what happens when you place a demand on the power of God within you.

Do not worry. God is writing your amazing story. He's out in front of you. Where God guides you, He will provide for you. Every detail of your life matters and is contributing to God's big picture.

In my weakness, God proved Himself strong. He is still using me in ways I never imagined.

Created for a Purpose

In the previous sections, I showed that God created you *on purpose* and He created you *with purpose*. In this section I'll help you see He created you *for a purpose*. You have a specific call on your life—a unique assignment, something you were born to accomplish that allows you to make God look good.

There was a time in the early days of my career as a recording artist when I compared my voice, my looks, and even my success to other Christian female singers. Looking back on that season of my life, I now realize that Satan, the enemy of my soul, was doing all he could to prevent me from carrying out God's purpose for my life. If he could keep me focused on myself and my shortcomings, then I wouldn't be focused on my purpose.

How many times have you compared yourself with someone else? Have you envied how another person looks, the way she wears her hair, or the clothes she wears? Let me say right here that comparison and competition are tools the adversary uses to distract you from your mission. So many women look in the mirror and think their worth and value is found in how they look on the outside. You may have said,

> If only I were thinner.
> I wish I could be a little taller.
> I wish I had her money.
> I wish I had her sense of humor.
> If I looked like her then others might accept and admire me.

But, my friend, God created you just the way He wanted you to be with the gifts and talents He wanted you to have. Your true identity is not in your looks. Your looks may be how people recognize you. But you find your identity on the inside where Christ lives. One verse I keep in mind is 1 Samuel 16:7, which says, "Man looks at the outward appearance, but the LORD looks at the heart."

People may admire your hair and your clothes. We all like nice things. We can appreciate a pretty house or a luxury car. However, the condition of your hair or your house doesn't impress God. He is more concerned about the condition of your heart.

When you turn your heart toward God, you'll find adventure in pursuing His plan. Ever since I can remember, I've wanted to be a singer. Growing up in the church and in the shadow of Motown, I naturally gravitated to music. But that was only the beginning. God had a greater purpose for me. Why? So I could chase after fame, awards, and popularity? I have a much bigger purpose. I have won my share of awards, and I am grateful for each one of them. Don't get me wrong—I am living my dream. But I don't sing for earthly awards. I sing for heavenly rewards. I sing for an audience of One.

Even at the stage of my life when many of my peers have retired, I really believe that my best days are still out there in front of me. I don't intend to retire; I want to re-fire. I have realized my dream of being a professional singer, but there is so much more to come. Today, I am singing, creating songs, writing books, and speaking to women, as well as teaching and mentoring singers and songwriters. I run an internet radio station at BabbieMasonRadio.com. I even went back to school and got my master's degree. At this age—I call it $69.95 plus tax, shipping, and handling—I find that there is no expiration date on God's plan for my life. At this season of my journey, I have learned a great life lesson. Let me share it with you: "Be yourself. Everybody else is taken!"

It doesn't matter how old you are or where you come from. You are God's masterpiece—a stunning success. Listen to what Ephesians 2:10 has to say about you: "We are his workmanship, created in Christ Jesus unto good works, which God hath before ordained that we should walk in them" (KJV).

Read the same passage from the Amplified Bible:

For we are His workmanship [His own master work, a work of art], created in Christ Jesus [reborn from above—spiritually transformed, renewed, ready to be used] for good works, which God prepared [for us] beforehand [taking paths which He set], so that we would walk in them [living the good life which He prearranged and made ready for us].

Read the passage again. This time, read each verse and place your name in the context of each promise.

_____, you are His workmanship.
     (Your name)

_____, you are His own master work, a work of art.
     (Your name)

_____, you are created in Christ Jesus [reborn from
     (Your name)
above—spiritually transformed, renewed, ready to be used] for good works, which God prepared beforehand.

_____, you are walking in them, living the good life.
     (Your name)

_____, God has prearranged all of this and made it
     (Your name)
ready for your use.

That is who you really are! You are a masterpiece, an expression of God's creativity, a work of art. God has not merely changed you, but He has also transformed you. You are renewed and ready to be used.

Use Your Gifts for God

My friend, you must learn to think of yourself as gifted. Why? Because God endowed you with a plethora of gifts. You must think of yourself as someone who has something to contribute to this world. Giftedness doesn't just apply to those of us in public ministry. Everyone possesses gifts and talents they can use to glorify God. Read the uplifting words from 1 Peter 4:10–11 (NLT) and take hold of the truth as it applies to your life.

> God has given each of you a gift from his great variety of spiritual gifts. Use them well to serve one another. Do you have the gift of speaking? Then speak as though God himself were speaking through you. Do you have the gift of helping others? Do it with all the strength and energy that God supplies. Then everything you do will bring glory to God through Jesus Christ. All glory and power to him forever and ever! Amen.

Can you say "Amen" to that? The sooner you embrace that truth, the sooner you can be about using your gifts to intimately express your worship for God and make Him look good on the earth. You'll find that using your gifts for God will result in His glory and your joy.

So how does understanding your purpose tie into shining your light and sharing your faith? I like using the phrase "making God look good" because that is actually what I mean. When people see you living for God, you can't help but shine and they can't help but be blessed. Even when times are hard, they can see how you respond to the low moments. They can observe for themselves how you respond to life's ups and downs. It should matter to you because now you know there is a call on your life. God has given you a reason for living. It matters to others because the light you shine will show them the way. And it matters to God because it brings Him great pleasure to see you living your life for Him. And that brings us back to a Scripture verse we discussed earlier in this chapter: "Thou art worthy, O Lord, to receive glory and honour and power: for thou hast created all things, and for thy pleasure they are and were created" (Rev. 4:11 KJV).

Many people have it all convoluted. They worship their work. They work at their play, and they play at their worship. But for the blood-bought daughter of the most high King, washing the clothes, feeding the baby, cleaning the shower, buying your friend a cup of coffee, going to church, praying for your family, and sharing your faith with others—everything you do is about worship.

Worship is a sacrifice of praise, like sweet-smelling incense to God. I saved the following story until the end of this book because it will help you remember that every effort on your part is a song of worship.

One of my relatives, a widow named Laura, was a resident in a senior adult care facility. Laura's ninety-fifth birthday fell on a Sunday, so that afternoon I paid her a surprise visit and brought her a gift basket. When I arrived at the care facility, she was in the large gathering room. We shared tears of joy as we embraced each other. I met her friends, nurses, and caretakers, and she gave me a tour of her cute apartment. I was happy to see she was enjoying good physical, mental, and emotional care.

After an hour or so, she guided me back to the lobby. We hugged and said our goodbyes. But as I was leaving, I couldn't help but notice the grand piano across the lobby. The instrument seemed to call my name. It was Sunday, after all, a day to give praise to God.

God placed a quick impulse in my heart, so I went to the front desk and asked the receptionist if I could play the piano. She said it was a great idea, and so I sat down at the piano and sang a favorite hymn.

I couldn't believe what happened next. Folks from all over the lobby gathered around the piano and joined in the singing. People in wheelchairs rolled their way up to participate. Those on walkers, canes, and crutches sang along as they formed a circle around the piano. Nurses and caregivers clapped and harmonized with the music. We lifted our voices together until the minister arrived to start the Sunday service.

A few months later, Laura passed away. I was honored to sing at her homegoing celebration. Much to my surprise, one of the caregivers who had been on duty the day of my previous visit spoke to me after the funeral. She recalled gathering around the piano and joining in the singing that Sunday afternoon. I'll never forget her words to me:

"You know, the day you came to visit Laura was one of the lowest days of my life. I was so discouraged and depressed. Then you sat down and began to sing and play the piano. I sensed God's presence in the room. Even while I was on my job, I worshipped God and gave Him thanks and praise for being so good to me. That day was my favorite day *ever* while I was on my job."

Do you understand what a privilege it was to hear her words? In a world of darkness and oppression, God has chosen you and me to represent His kingdom of light. In everything we do and say, God has handpicked us to point others to Him. You see, when your whole life is an act of worship, your greatest moments in God's presence don't even have to be inside of a church. You can worship God at home, in the grocery store, in a restaurant, or even at an assisted living facility for senior adults. In this sense, evangelism is not about the work but about the worship.

> **You are not loved
> for who you are.
> You are loved for
> whose you are.**

Yes, your occupation is important. But listen closely: Your job does not define who you are. I happen to be a singer, songwriter, and author. But if I don't sing another song or write another chapter of a book, I still have value, worth, and purpose. The same holds true for you. Your occupation does not define your purpose. Your relationship with Jesus defines your purpose. You are not loved for who you are. You are loved for whose you are.

Read the second verse of the song I wrote that inspired the title of this book, *Each One Reach One*:

The message is unchanging, go ye into all the world
And share your love for Jesus, far away and door to door
Just like somebody told you,
That Jesus loves you so
You can tell someone, who will tell someone
Until the whole world knows

You are not alone in your quest to turn on and turn up your light. I am with you in the Spirit. Others who will read this book are with us too. Together, we will combine our efforts to share the love of Jesus and make a difference in the world.

As you understand Christ's call more clearly, your heart will fill with confidence. Indeed, God created you to "let your light so shine before men, that they may see your good works and glorify your Father in heaven." Shine then, in such a way that everything you do brings glory to God. That is real worship.

God has given us this opportunity at this time in history to know Him and make Him known. Psalm 100:5 says, "The LORD is good; His mercy is everlasting, and His truth endures to all generations." Sharing the gospel message to all generations sounds like a lofty goal. But it's possible to reach the world when we all do our part. Could we endeavor to do this as we embark upon this new adventure in sharing our faith? Let's pray together that the second verse and chorus of "Each One Reach One" will ring true.

———————————◆———————————

Bridge
Will you go and labor
Will you hold high your light
One by one and two by two
We can win our world for Jesus Christ

Chorus
Each one can reach one
As we follow after Christ, we all can lead one
We can lead one to the Savior
Then together we can tell the world
That Jesus is the way
If we, each one, reach one[3]

———————————◆———————————

Reflections

1. After reading the chapter, in what ways can you "make God look good" by shining your light?

2. Think about your God-given gifts and talents. What unique gifts are "in your hand" right now?

3. In what ways can you nurture the gifts God has given you?

4. When you use your gifts for God, in what ways does your heart feel encouraged? How do others respond when you use your gifts to bless them?

5. How does using your gifts in service of Christ increase your faith in Him?

6. What is something you would do for God if you weren't afraid of failing?

7. What was the boldest action you took for the sake of the gospel in the last month?

8. Worship doesn't have to take place in a church building. How can you practice the presence of God in your everyday life?

Prayer of Salvation and Memory Verses

The Bible says every person has sinned and falls short of what it takes to please a holy God (Rom. 3:23). Because our hearts are sinful, we need a Savior. That's why God sent His Son, Jesus. Accepting Jesus means you accept the sacrifice Jesus made for your sins. You are saved from sin, and you are saved to enjoy your relationship with God.

Regardless of who you are, you matter to God. He created you so He could love you. He loves you now, and He wants you to love Him back. He knows you and, in return, He wants you to know Him. This is not based on religion. It's based on an intimate relationship of faith, trust, and obedience—one you can begin right now. John 3:16 says, "For God so loved the world that He gave His only begotten Son, that whoever believes in Him should not perish but have everlasting life."

But God will not force His way into your life. You must welcome Him by inviting His Son, Jesus, into your heart and life to be your Lord and Savior. Jesus said, "Look! I stand at the door and knock. If you hear my voice and open the door, I will come in, and we will share a meal together as friends" (Rev. 3:20 NLT). In other words, Jesus wants to fellowship with you every day from now on. When you invite Jesus to be your Savior, three things will take place: (1) your past sins will be forgiven, (2) every day of your life will have a purpose, and (3) you will have an eternal home in heaven.

Don't worry if you don't feel different. It doesn't matter if you don't understand all the answers. God just wants you to walk by faith and grow in your relationship with Him. Are you ready to pray now? Simply pray this prayer or use your own words. Mean it with all your heart.

> Dear God, right now, I know I need You. I confess my sin and my need for You in my life. I believe Your Son, Jesus, was crucified, that He died, and that He rose again for my sin. I invite Jesus to come into my life to be my Lord and Savior. I want to be the person You created me to be. I long to fulfill Your purpose for my life from this moment on. Thank You, Lord, for saving me. Amen.

Friend, if you sincerely prayed that prayer, you are now a Christian. Welcome to the family of God. As soon as you can, please share your decision with your pastor, your parents, your spouse, or a friend.

Memory Verses by Chapter

Introduction: You are the light of the world—like a city on a hilltop that cannot be hidden. No one lights a lamp and then puts it under a basket. Instead, a lamp is placed on a stand, where it gives light to everyone in the house. (Matthew 5:14–15 NLT)

Chapter 1: For God so loved the world that He gave His only begotten Son, that whoever believes in Him should not perish but have everlasting life. (John 3:16)

Chapter 2: Let your light so shine before men, that they may see your good works and glorify your Father in heaven. (Matthew 5:16)

Chapter 3: The fruit of the Spirit is love, joy, peace, patience, kindness, goodness, faithfulness, gentleness, self-control; against such things there is no law. (Galatians 5:22–23 ESV)

Chapter 4: Then Jesus came to them and said, "All authority in heaven and on earth has been given to me. Therefore go and make disciples of all nations, baptizing them in the name of the Father and of the Son and of the Holy Spirit, and teaching them to obey everything I have commanded you. And surely I am with you always, to the very end of the age." (Matthew 28:18–20 NIV)

Chapter 5: So speak encouraging words to one another. Build up hope so you'll all be together in this, no one left out, no one left behind. I know you're already doing this; just keep on doing it. (1 Thessalonians 5:11 MSG)

Chapter 6: Blessed is the one who perseveres under trial because, having stood the test, that person will receive the crown of life that the Lord has promised to those who love him. (James 1:12 NIV)

Chapter 7: And do not be conformed to this world, but be transformed by the renewing of your mind, that you may prove what is that good and acceptable and perfect will of God. (Romans 12:2)

Chapter 8: "For I know the plans I have for you," declares the LORD, "plans to prosper you and not to harm you, plans to give you hope and a future. Then you will call on me and come and pray to me, and I will listen to you. You will seek me and find me when you seek me with all your heart." (Jeremiah 29:11–13 NIV)

Acknowledgments

Every writer depends on a team to help get their book across the finish line. I'm grateful to so many for their contribution.

To my husband, Charles: You're my biggest cheerleader and constant encourager. You ate way too much drive-through and curbside to-go meals while I wrote this book. Home-cooked meals are on the way. I promise.

To my siblings, Ben, Al, Benita, and Matt: I must always give you a shout-out and your props. Much love to all of you, "Reverend Wade's children." March forth!

In memory of my parents, Pastor Willie George Wade (1922–1987) and Georgie Mae Stephen Wade (1923–2015): Although you are both in heaven now, your words still ring true: "If God be your partner, make your plans larger." I will always remember your love and the great heritage of faith that I embrace and gladly pass on to others.

To Sherri and Morgan: Thanks so much for keeping all the plates spinning at Babbie Mason Ministries. You're the best!

To Pastor John Hull, friends, and family at Eastside Baptist Church, Marietta, Georgia: Who would've thought that life and ministry would end up coming full circle? It's a blessing to be back where it all began.

To Pastor Everett Spencer, friends, and family at New Dimensions Church, Newnan, Georgia: Thank you for demonstrating what it looks like to serve God and people with joy. You have taught us well.

To Susan McPherson, my editor at David C Cook: Thank you for answering the phone! Your passion for Christ is super contagious. It's an honor to do life with you during this season.

To everyone on the David C Cook Publishing team: The word *amazing* is so overused. But that is the word I use to describe all of you. Thank you for contributing your keen abilities to the success of this book. It is a blessing to work with all of you.

To you, the reader: If our world ever needed you to shine your light for Christ, it's now. I wrote this book to encourage and inspire you to raise the light of Jesus higher. Start right there in the world where you are. I'm cheering you on, dear friend. Shine on!

Saving the best for last: Thank You to my Lord and Savior, Jesus Christ. On that day when I meet You face to face, I hope that I would not have a single gift, talent, or skill left but I could say to You, "Heaven and earth will soon be passed. But only what I did for Christ will last. And it was only for the cause of Christ." May Your name be praised. Amen.

Notes

Introduction

1. Jason Perry, *A Word to the Wise* (South Holland, IL: Oak Tree Leadership, 2023), 91.

Chapter 1: Your Time to Shine

1. The verses alluded to in this paragraph are Genesis 1:3–4, 14–19; 1 John 1:4–5.

2. James Hastings, ed., *Dictionary of the Bible* (London: T&T Clark, 1914), 247.

3. "Each One Reach One," lyrics and music by Babbie Mason, on *With All My Heart*, Word Music, 1990.

Chapter 2: Surrender Your Light

1. Moody Bible Institute, "D. L. Moody: Meet Dwight," accessed December 18, 2023, www.moody.edu/about/our-bold-legacy/d-l-moody.

2. Jean Priestap, "It All Started with a Sunday School Teacher," *Vision for Christ* (blog), March 8, 2017, https://visionforchristworld.com/it-started-with-a-sunday-school-teacher.

3. Elijah P. Brown, *The Real Billy Sunday: The Life and Works of Rev. William Ashley Sunday* (Grand Rapids, MI: Fleming H. Revell, 1914).

4. "Common Reference Questions," Wheaton College, accessed January 16, 2024, www.wheaton.edu /about-wheaton/museum-and-collections/wheaton-archives-and-special-collections/services/ reference-services/common-reference-questions.

5. "The Amazing Story of God's Ambassador," Billy Graham Library, accessed January 16, 2024, https://billygrahamlibrary.org/billy-graham.

6. *Merriam-Webster Dictionary* (online), s.v. "everything," accessed January 25, 2024, www.merriam-webster.com/dictionary/everything.

7. Oxford Languages, s.v. "let," accessed January 16, 2024, www.google.com/search?q=let+definition&rlz= 1C1CHBD_enUS942US942&oq=let+definition&gs_lcrp=EgZjaHJvbWUyDggAEEUYJxg5GIAEGI- oFMgwIARAAGBQYhwIYgAQyBwgCEAAYgAQyBwgDEAAYgAQyBwgEEAAYgAQyBggFEEUYPDI GCAYQRRg9MgYIBxBFGEHSAQkxNjMxMxOWowajeoAgCwAgA&sourceid=chrome&ie=UTF-8.

8. *Merriam-Webster Dictionary*, s.v. "humility," accessed November 14, 2023, www.merriam-webster.com/dictionary/humility.

9. Rick Warren, *The Purpose-Driven Life* (Grand Rapids, MI: Zondervan, 2002), 148.

10. Rich Berry (Atlanta city advisor, Navigators), in discussion with the author, September 27, 2023.

11. "With All My Heart," lyrics and music by Babbie Mason, on *With All My Heart*, Word Music, 1990.

Chapter 3: Own Your Light

1. Max Lucado, *A Gentle Thunder: Hearing God through the Storm* (Nashville, TN: Word Publishing, 1995), 155.

2. John Newton, "Amazing Grace," 1772, public domain; Horace Clarence Boyer, ed., "Amazing Grace," *Lift Every Voice and Sing II: An African American Hymnal* (New York: Church Publishing, 1993), hymn no. 181.

3. Dan Hart, "Kindness: The Glue That Holds Marriages Together," Family Research Council, February 11, 2021, www.frc.org/blog/2021/02/kindness-glue-holds-marriages-together.

4. Heather V. MacArthur, "Kindness at Work: The New Link to Engagement and Performance," *Forbes*, June 5, 2023, www.forbes.com/sites/hvmacarthur/2023/06/05/kindness-at-work-the-new-link-to -engagement-and-performance.

5. Andrew Swinand, "Why Kindness at Work Pays Off," *Harvard Business Review*, July 21, 2023, https://hbr.org/2023/07/why-kindness-at-work-pays-off.

6. "How to Hire the Right Employees to Grow Your Business," Lee Group, accessed February 12, 2024, https://theleegroup.com/hire-right-employees-grow-business/#:~:text=Good%20employees%20who%20 are%20happy,influences%20a%20company's%20financial%20performance.

7. Cedars-Sinai Staff, "The Science of Kindness," Cedars Sinai Blog, February 13, 2019, www.cedars-sinai.org /blog/science-of-kindness.html.

8. David A. Fryburg, "Kindness as a Stress Reduction—Health Promotion Intervention: A Review of the Psychobiology of Caring," *American Journal of Lifestyle Medicine* 16, no. 1 (2022): 89–100, www.ncbi.nlm .nih.gov/pmc/articles/PMC8848115.

9. Jessica Brodie, "What Does the Greek Word Kairos Mean in the Bible?," Crosswalk.com (blog), March 26, 2021, www.crosswalk.com/faith/bible-study/what-does-the-greek-word-kairos-mean-in-the-bible.html.

10. Thayer's Greek Lexicon, s.v. "kairos," BibleHub, https://biblehub.com/greek/2540.htm.

Chapter 4: Turn Up Your Light

1. Unless otherwise noted, all facts are gleaned from Elisabeth Elliot, *Through Gates of Splendor: 50th Anniversary Edition* (Carol Stream, IL: Tyndale, 2015).

2. For the use of the word *Waodani*, see Russell T. Hitt, *Jungle Pilot* (Grand Rapids, MI: Discovery House, 1959), 176.

3. Hitt, *Jungle Pilot*.

4. Ivan Mesa, "The Missionary Legacy of Jim and Elisabeth Elliot," International Mission Board (IMB), April 1, 2019, www.imb.org/2019/04/01/missionary-legacy-jim-elisabeth-elliot/#:~:text=They%20sought%2C%20along%20with%20four,on%20the%20modern%20missions%20movement.

5. "51% of Churchgoers Don't Know of the Great Commission," Barna, March 27, 2018, www.barna.com/research/half-churchgoers-not-heard-great-commission.

6. "51% of Churchgoers Don't Know."

7. King James Bible Dictionary, s.v. "go," accessed March 26, 2024, https://kingjamesbibledictionary.com/Dictionary/go.

8. Vocabulary.com, s.v. "go," accessed December 20, 2023, www.vocabulary.com/dictionary/go.

9. Oxford Languages, s.v. "so," accessed January 16, 2024, www.google.com/search?sca_esv=725712b13be26739&rlz=1C1CHBD_enUS942US942&sxsrf=ACQVn09906xo56wCl1mdKkCXHjNy6iVzkQ:1707941480490&q=so&si=AKbGX_pjtwRxhbBXmwtBf7cl9usFWcVNiRa9QSWUrHqQsXn_YOPfNgi4TFYQzEp9oogkQPkn6u4mKMAw0YNDo4Ew9GytfZCRjg%3D%3D&expnd=1&sa=X&ved=2ahUKEwjpmPfp0auEAxWTkYkEHUlFCEgQ2v4IegQIFBBr&biw=724&bih=656&dpr=1.

10. *Cambridge Dictionary*, s.v. "so," accessed February 14, 2024, https://dictionary.cambridge.org/us/dictionary/english/so.

11. *Collins Dictionary*, s.v. "integer," www.collinsdictionary.com/us/dictionary/english/integer.

12. *Collins Dictionary*, s.v. "integrity," www.collinsdictionary.com/us/dictionary/english/integrity.

13. Deborah Pegues, "Empowering Women to Take Control of Their Finances," Focus on the Family Broadcast, September 10, 2019, reposted October 9, 2023, www.focusonthefamily.com/episodes/broadcast/empowering-women-to-take-control-of-their-finances.

14. Myles Munroe, "Dr. Myles Munroe: The Power of Integrity," November 18, 2019, YouTube video, 2:12, www.youtube.com/watch?v=nKGjZ9PTMZs.

15. *Noah Webster's First Edition of an American Dictionary of the English Language*, s.v. "holy" (Chesapeake, VA: Foundation for American Christian Education, 1828).

16. Elliot, *Through Gates of Splendor*, 8.

17. Charles Stanley, *God's Way Day by Day* (Nashville, TN: J. Countryman, 2004), 90.

Chapter 5: Give Your Light Away

1. Philip Yancey, *Where Is God When It Hurts?* (New York: Walker/Zondervan, 1988), 262.

2. Vocabulary.com, s.v. "engaged," accessed October 30, 2023, www.vocabulary.com/dictionary/engaged.

3. Yancey, *Where Is God When It Hurts?*, 262.

4. "Humpty Dumpty" in *The Little Golden Mother Goose* (Racine, WI: Western, 1957), 10.

5. "He'll Find a Way," lyrics and music by Donna Douglas, on *Praise Celebration*, Word Records, 1997.

6. "Love Like That," lyrics and music by Donna Douglas and Babbie Mason, on *This I Know for Sure*, Mason Hill Music Group, 2013.

Chapter 6: Can I Get a Witness?

1. Larry J. Michael, *Spurgeon on Leadership: Key Insights for Christian Leaders from the Prince of Preachers* (Grand Rapids, MI: Kregel, 2010), 87.

2. Pastor Jim Cymbala, in conversation with the author, June 2023.

3. "Love Is the More Excellent Way," lyrics and music by Babbie Mason and Turner Lawton, on *Heritage of Faith*, Word Records, 1996.

4. "Show Me How to Love," lyrics and music by Babbie Mason, on *Carry On*, Word Music, 1988.

Chapter 7: Doing Good

1. Albert Pike, *Words from the Heart Spoken of His Dead Brethren* (Charleston, SC: Scottish Rite of Freemasonry, 1899), 11.

2. This summary of Martin Luther's theology is found in Steven D. Paulson, *Luther for Armchair Theologians* (Louisville, KY: Presbyterian Publishing Corporation, 2004), 182.

3. *Merriam-Webster*, s.v. "abide," www.merriam-webster.com/dictionary/abide.

4. Carolyn Massiah, "We Should All Strive to Be the Palm in the Storm," UCFToday (University of Central Florida News), September 7, 2016, www.ucf.edu/news/we-all-should-strive-to-be-the-palm-in-the-storm.

5. Oxford Languages, s.v. "lavish," accessed December 20, 2023, www.google.com/search?q=definition+of+lavish&client=ms-android-verizon-us-rvc3&sourceid=chrome-mobile&ie=UTF-8&inm=vs#tts=0.

6. C. Gregg Carlson and Graig Reicks, "Estimating Corn Yields," in *South Dakota State University Extension, iGrow Corn: Best Management Practices* (Vermillion, SD: South Dakota Board of Regents, 2019), Table 38.2, https://extension.sdstate.edu/sites/default/files/2019-09/S-0003-38-Corn.pdf. See also "Corn FAQs," Iowa Corn, accessed February 15, 2024, www.iowacorn.org/education/faqs#:~:text=How%20many%20kernels%20are%20there,in%20an%20acre%20of%20corn.

7. Gwen Costello, *Spiritual Gems from Mother Teresa* (New London, CT: Twenty-Third Publications, 2008), 3.

Chapter 8: Making God Look Good

1. "What Is Worship?," Worship Basic 101, accessed December 21, 2023, https://sites.google.com/site/worshipbasic101/about-praise--worship/what-is-worship.

2. Charles R. Swindoll, *Growing Strong in the Seasons of Life* (Portland, OR: Multnomah, 1983), 352.

3. "Each One Reach One," lyrics and music by Babbie Mason, on *With All My Heart*, Word Music, 1990.

Bible Credits

Unless otherwise noted, all Scripture quotations are taken from the New King James Version®. Copyright © 1982 by Thomas Nelson. Used by permission. All rights reserved.

Scripture quotations marked AMP are taken from the Amplified® Bible (AMP), Copyright © 2015 by The Lockman Foundation. Used by permission. www.lockman.org.

CEV are taken from the Contemporary English Version © 1991, 1995 by American Bible Society. Used by Permission.

ESV are taken from the ESV® Bible (The Holy Bible, English Standard Version®), copyright © 2001 by Crossway, a publishing ministry of Good News Publishers. Used by permission. All rights reserved.

KJV are taken from the King James Version of the Bible. (Public Domain.)

TLB are taken from The Living Bible copyright © 1971. Used by permission of Tyndale House Publishers, Carol Stream, Illinois 60188. All rights reserved.

Be the first to know about Babbie's new books,
music releases and tour schedule
when you visit Babbie's website at **Babbie.com**
and subscribe to Babbie's e-newsletter.
At the website, you'll also find
every issue of Babbie's Blog, new videos,
photos from the road and updates on *The Inner Circle*,
a weekend seminar for Christian creatives
who want to hone their skills in the areas of
launching music ministry, singing, songwriting,
authoring books, and public speaking.

VISIT BABBIE.COM TODAY

babbiemason**radio** ▶

Ready for a refreshing change in Christian music radio?

Make **BabbieMasonRadio.com**
your new online music destination.
This exciting internet platform
is a unique and refreshing place
where your favorite Christian
and Gospel music can be heard.

What makes Babbie Mason Radio so unique?

You'll hear the complete and expansive library
of Babbie's music, devotions, and stories behind her songs,
along with music artists from your favorite genres
like Kirk Franklin, Maverick City Music,
Cece Winans, Phil Wickham and Tamela Mann.
The platform also features the voices of many
of your favorite Bible study teachers such as
Charles Stanley, Tony Evans, Crawford Loritts,
Priscilla Shirer, Max Lucado and more.

On the web 24/7/365,
Babbie Mason Radio plays the latest
Christian music in a format that is encouraging,
informative, family-friendly and God-honoring.
At home or on the go, BabbieMasonRadio.com
is the place on the internet where you
can find hope in Christ at the click of a button.

babbiemason**radio**.com